"Better than getting hit on the head with a bushel of apples."
Isaac Newton

"Tremendous book but I bet no one will buy it."
Arthur Schopenhauer

"I'll take that bet!" *Blaise Pascal*

"A wake-up call!" *Immanuel Kant*

"A *complete* triumph!" *Kurt Godel*

"It will make you smarter than you think." *Ludwig Wittgenstein*

YOU'VE GOT TO BE KIDDING!

HOW JOKES CAN HELP YOU THINK

JOHN CAPPS AND DONALD CAPPS

WILEY-BLACKWELL

A John Wiley & Sons, Ltd., Publication

This edition first published 2009
© 2009 John Capps and Donald Capps

Blackwell Publishing was acquired by John Wiley & Sons in February 2007. Blackwell's publishing program has been merged with Wiley's global Scientific, Technical, and Medical business to form Wiley-Blackwell.

Registered Office
John Wiley & Sons Ltd, The Atrium, Southern Gate, Chichester, West Sussex, PO19 8SQ, United Kingdom

Editorial Offices
350 Main Street, Malden, MA 02148-5020, USA
9600 Garsington Road, Oxford, OX4 2DQ, UK
The Atrium, Southern Gate, Chichester, West Sussex, PO19 8SQ, UK

For details of our global editorial offices, for customer services, and for information about how to apply for permission to reuse the copyright material in this book please see our website at www.wiley.com/wiley-blackwell.

The right of John Capps and Donald Capps to be identified as the author of this work has been asserted in accordance with the Copyright, Designs and Patents Act 1988.

Wiley also publishes its books in a variety of electronic formats. Some content that appears in print may not be available in electronic books.

Designations used by companies to distinguish their products are often claimed as trademarks. All brand names and product names used in this book are trade names, service marks, trademarks or registered trademarks of their respective owners. The publisher is not associated with any product or vendor mentioned in this book. This publication is designed to provide accurate and authoritative information in regard to the subject matter covered. It is sold on the understanding that the publisher is not engaged in rendering professional services. If professional advice or other expert assistance is required, the services of a competent professional should be sought.

Library of Congress Cataloging-in-Publication Data

Capps, John M., 1970–
    You've got to be kidding! : how jokes can help you think / John Capps and Donald Capps.
        p.   cm.
    Includes bibliographical references and index.
    ISBN 978-1-4051-9665-9 (hardcover : alk. paper) – ISBN 978-1-4051-9664-2 (pbk. : alk. paper)
    1. Critical thinking. 2. Wit and humor. I. Capps, Donald. II. Title.
    BC177.C3455 2009
    160–dc22

                                        2009007418

A catalogue record for this book is available from the British Library.

Set in 10.5/13pt Minion by SPi Publisher Services, Pondicherry, India
Printed in the United States of America, by Sheridan Books, Inc.

2   2009

On the first day of school, the kindergarten teacher said, "If anyone has to go to the bathroom, hold up two fingers." A little voice from the back of the room asked, "How will that help?"

Contents

Preface

This book came about through a happy confluence of seemingly unrelated events. One of us, a psychologist, was writing a book on humor, and stumbled onto Ted Cohen's *Jokes: Philosophical Thoughts on Joking Matters* (1999). He told the other, a philosopher, about the book, and this led both to begin thinking about collaborating on a book on humor. Our initial idea was to write a book in psychology, one that would combine humor, cognitive therapy, and philosophy. Then, however, the fact that the philosopher was teaching undergraduate courses in logic and critical thinking led us to think that a philosophy book would be more useful.

This idea was exciting to the psychologist because he thought it would be nice to contribute to a philosophy book. It was also daunting because, although he had been an undergraduate philosophy major, this was many years ago, and he had forgotten much of what he had learned in logic courses. Then, however, he discovered Jamie Whyte's *Crimes against Logic* (2005). The back cover identified Whyte as a past lecturer of philosophy at Cambridge University and winner of a philosophy journal's prize for the best article by a philosopher under thirty. The words "past" and "under thirty" suggested that the author and the psychologist-reader had certain life experiences in common. More importantly, the subtitle – *Exposing the Bogus Arguments of Politicians, Priests, Journalists, and Other Serial Offenders* – suggested that the book would enable him to pick up where he had left off years ago. After reading it, he sent off a proposed set of chapter headings to the philosopher who responded with a carefully formulated table of contents. The project was now underway.

As we were writing the book, another book appeared on the philosophy shelves of local bookstores: *Plato and a Platypus Walk into a Bar: Understanding Philosophy through Jokes* (Cathcart and Klein, 2007). The book cover indicated that the authors, Thomas Cathcart and Daniel Klein, had majored in philosophy at Harvard and had then gone on to pursue other, quite unrelated careers. The book's appearance caused the psychologist, who should have known better, several sleepless nights: "Cathcart and Klein got there first," he moaned to the philosopher. The philosopher, however, remained calm and unperturbed and cited the following joke:

> The train conductor was going through the cars collecting tickets. He came to the seat where a woman was sitting with her son. "Ma'am," he asked, "how old is your little boy?" "He's four." "He looks at least twelve to me." "He worries a lot."

He also pointed out that the Cathcart and Klein book has ten chapters, only one of which is devoted to logic, and this chapter considers only two of the twenty-three fallacies we were covering in our book. He concluded that, if anything, we should be elated that others have paved the way for our book on jokes and critical thinking. Thus mollified, the psychologist took his subsequent discovery of *Stop Me If You've Heard This: A History and Philosophy of Jokes* by Jim Holt (2008) with remarkable serenity. What's especially noteworthy here is that the philosopher countered the emotional reaction of the psychologist with an appeal to reason supported by compelling evidence.

As John Morreall's *The Philosophy of Laughter and Humor* (1987) shows, philosophers have been interested in humor throughout the history of philosophy. Our book, however, has a special affinity with the investigative spirit of Henri Bergson's *Laughter* (1912). Bergson sought answers to these questions: What does laughter mean? And what is the "basal element" in the laughable? He knew that gaining answers to these questions would be an uphill battle. After all, "The greatest thinkers, from Aristotle downward, have tackled this little problem, which has a knack of baffling every effort, of slipping away and escaping only to bob up again, a pert challenge flung at philosophic speculation" (p. 1). However, his excuse for attacking the problem anew was that he would not try to imprison the comic spirit within a definition, but instead treat it with the respect due any product of human imagination. By establishing "a practical, intimate acquaintance" with it, he would honor the fact that "the comic spirit has a logic of its own, even in its wildest eccentricities," that it "has a method in its madness" (p. 2).

On the basis of this intimate acquaintance for nearly two hundred pages, Bergson concluded that the comic spirit has all the appearances of being logical, but it actually abandons logic (p. 196). Similarly, Ted Cohen writes about a type of joke that it displays "a crazy logic," "an insane rationality," "a logical rigor gone over the edge," and involves "twisted reasoning" (p. 46). So, we think it makes a lot of sense for a philosopher and a psychologist to collaborate on a book about jokes and critical thinking. We agree that jokes often reflect the abandonment of logic and reason. We also believe, however, that some jokes make a lot of sense. The fact that some do and some don't is precisely what makes them a valuable resource for critical thinking.

Acknowledgements

A couple of professors can put together what they would like to think is a publishable manuscript but it takes many other professionals, working together, to convert a manuscript into a book. The names of many of these persons are unknown to the authors. Of those whose names are known to us, we are especially grateful to Jeff Dean, philosophy editor at Wiley-Blackwell, who expressed interest in our manuscript and shepherded it through the review process. Also, in a moment of sheer inspiration, he came up with the book's title and subtitle. Thoroughly impressed with his title, we have long since forgotten our own. Tiffany Mok attended to the various issues that kept the publication process moving along, and made certain that we were consulted on all aspects of the preparation of the book, including the cover design. Graeme Leonard did a splendid job in the actual editing of the manuscript. Among those whose names are unknown to us, we want to express our particular thanks to the reviewers of our original manuscript. We aren't kidding when we say that we took their criticisms and suggestions very seriously. We and our readers are the beneficiaries of both.

Also, writing a book like this requires telling a lot of jokes and we'd like to thank the people, willing and unwilling, who listened and told us what was funny and what wasn't. We found ourselves depending particularly on the good sense of humor, and also the good sense and good humor, of Evelyn Brister and Karen Capps, as we tested the jokes for this book. We are solely responsible for the bad jokes that remain!

Finally, we have noticed that in the case of some coauthored books one author will dedicate it to one person and the other author will dedicate it to another person. In our case, we both dedicate this book to Eamon Capps, our son and grandson. At three years of age, he has already shown his impeccable sense of humor by finding most of what we do hilarious. Of course, if this book is right, then he may also be showing his critical thinking skills by laughing at our own shortcomings. So it is with joy, and a little guilt, that we welcome him into this family of joke-lovers.

Good Point!

Humor today goes hand in hand with our rationality, and not just rationality in the sense of cognitive sophistication, but also in the sense of a rational attitude toward the world. Part of this attitude is viewing things critically, and people with a well-developed sense of humor naturally look at things critically, because they are looking for incongruity.

John Morreall

Bad Limerick!!

A candid Professor confesses
That the secret of half his success is
Not his science, as such,
Nor its marvels so much
As his bright irresponsible guesses.

Thomas Thorneley

1 Why Thinking Critically Is Important

Critical thinking is about examining the reasons we give for what we believe. It is also about communicating in a clear, understandable, and reasonable way. Technically speaking, critical thinking is rational thinking. The word "rational" implies the ability to reason logically and usually means that one avoids emotionalism, i.e., appealing to one's feelings or intuitions as the basis for a particular belief. In practical terms, critical thinking involves being "reasonable," or having defensible reasons for what we believe and say. The word "reasonable" may imply the use of practical reason in making decisions and choices, and in this sense, critical thinking is relevant to solving problems. In this book, we will be using both terms – "rational" and "reasonable" – depending on the context.

We will also use the word "irrational" to refer to beliefs and actions that are illogical. Sometimes the word "irrational" is used as a synonym for saying or doing something in a strongly emotional manner. We will use the word "irrational" here in the more limited sense of engaging in faulty reasoning. This means that just because someone speaks or writes in a highly emotional manner does not necessarily mean that the belief itself is irrational, and, conversely, merely because someone speaks in a calm and measured way does not necessarily mean that the belief expressed is rational. The "emotionalism" that is being called into question here is where one appeals to one's emotions and, in effect, ignores or rejects evidence that challenges the validity of the belief in question.

Jokes make good illustrations of the logical fallacies that are a regular feature of critical thinking courses. Figuring out which logical fallacy a joke illustrates can be a valuable exercise in critical thinking. We will present jokes that illustrate these fallacies in chapters 2–5. We realize that by using jokes to illustrate critical thinking we risk undermining the importance of critical thinking, but we hope that this illustrative use of jokes will enable our readers to take the goals of critical thinking even more seriously than they might otherwise and also to get the informal fallacies better fixed in their minds than would otherwise be the case. If critical thinking is about examining the reasons people have for what they believe, then jokes are an especially engaging and memorable way of showing how these reasons can fall short. And if critical thinking is about being able to communicate in ways that are clear, understandable and reasonable, this often means avoiding the logical fallacies that create confusion and undermine honest dialogue, and because jokes commit these fallacies, they can help us learn where our communicating goes wrong.

The Relevance of Context

In this chapter we will discuss several aspects of what is involved in thinking and behaving in a rational manner. One of these concerns the issue of context. A belief or behavior can make sense in one context but not make sense in another. Here's an example of a joke in which someone does something that would be perfectly rational in another context but is essentially irrational in the context in which he currently finds himself:

> Two guys are walking down the street when a mugger approaches them and demands their money. They both grudgingly pull out their wallets and begin taking out their cash. Just then one guy turns to the other and hands him a bill. "Here's that $20 I owe you," he says.

It's doubtful that anyone would ever *really* pay back a debt in this way. But the joke illustrates the incongruity between the guy's rational behavior – paying back a loan – and the context in which he pays it back. He suddenly realizes that, since he's being robbed anyway, he might as well pay off a debt at the same time. Here's a joke that plays on the same incongruity:

> A New York cabbie is cruising near 5th Avenue when he picks up a man who wants to go to the Palmer House Hotel in Chicago. After a great deal of haggling the cabbie agrees to drive the man to Chicago, which takes them out of Manhattan, into New Jersey, across Pennsylvania, Ohio, and Indiana, and finally many hours later onto Lake Shore Drive to the Palmer House. The cabbie drives up to the main entrance, the man gives the cabbie several hundred dollars to cover the ride, and opens the door and gets out. Just then two women slide into the backseat and one says,

"We want to go to Shea Stadium." "No way, lady," the cabbie replies, "I don't go to Queens."

What the cabbie tells the lady makes sense to him – "I limit myself to Manhattan" – but it doesn't make much sense in a context where he is deadheading back to New York City from Chicago.

Differentiating the Rational from the Irrational

As these two examples show, jokes can upset our intuitions about what is rational and what is irrational. In the crazy sorts of situations jokes describe, it isn't always clear what is rational or irrational. Thus, jokes can help us recognize that we don't always have a clear grasp on what is rational. They are often a gentle reminder that we aren't always good judges of what is rational or irrational. Take this joke:

> Two friends decide to take an expensive fishing trip to Montana but after a week of fishing they only manage to catch one fish. So, on the way home one friend says to the other, "The way I figure it, that fish cost us $5,000." "Yeah," his friend replies, "Good thing we didn't catch more."

Here the irrationality is obvious and apparent. The second guy's reply might sound rational at first but it doesn't take more than a second to realize it isn't. Someone who says, "The guy's right. Two fish would cost $10,000" doesn't get the fact that his thinking isn't rational. Here's another one:

> A guy was hired to paint the line down the center of the road. The first day he managed to paint two miles, and his boss was very pleased. The next day he painted only 200 yards, but his boss thought he'd probably worked too hard the first day and needed to take it easier the second day. But on the third day he was only able to paint twenty feet. The boss called him into the office and demanded an explanation. The guy replied, "Well, you see it's getting so darned far to walk all the way back to the paint bucket."

Here, too, the irrationality is obvious. It also has practical consequences. Because he acted irrationally he'll probably lose his job. In real life the irrationality is *usually* more subtle but there are still practical consequences. So we should care about being rational because irrational thinking can have negative practical consequences.

One way of being irrational is to believe something that is obviously false. Say that two guys are hiking in the Rockies and one says to the other, "I'll bet you 10 bucks that I can jump across that 50-foot ravine," and the other guy replies, "You're on." So the first guy leaps to his death. As he falls, he might shout, "The joke's on you because I don't even have ten bucks!" But that's irrelevant. Because it's obviously impossible to leap across a 50-foot ravine, it is irrational to believe that one can. On the other hand, believing that he can leap across an 8-foot ravine is certainly conceivable, especially with a running start. It's even possible that believing he can do it would make a crucial difference to his success. But acting on an obviously false belief is irrational, and we shouldn't be surprised if it has negative consequences.

Another way of being irrational is to believe or say things that are contradictory. This can also have practical consequences. Here's an example:

> The manager of a baseball team went to his doctor to get an ulcer treated. "Remember" the doctor told him, "Don't get excited, don't get angry, and forget all about baseball when you're off the field. Try to remember it's just a game." "Thanks, Doc, I'll follow your advice." "Good. I'll see you in a month to find out how you're doing." As the patient heads to the door, the doctor says, "Oh, one more thing: why the hell did you let the pitcher bat for himself last night when you had men on first and third?"

Here the doctor contradicts himself and the patient has every right to accuse him of being irrational. Moreover, the doctor has spoiled whatever good he hoped to do.

Most of us try to be rational, at least, when we want others to think we know what we're talking about. Nearly everyone who holds contradictory beliefs *thinks* he or she is being rational: like the fisherman, the painter, and the doctor, it just hasn't dawned on them that they are actually thinking irrationally. So we aren't always good judges of whether we are rational or not. Jokes are one way of keeping this in mind.

> Bob received a parrot for his birthday. The parrot was fully grown, with a bad attitude and worse vocabulary. Every other word was an expletive, and the parrot was constantly cursing and swearing. Bob tried to change the bird's attitude by setting a good example, but the bird continued to swear as much as ever. This went on for several months until finally, in a moment of desperation, Bob put the parrot in the freezer. For a few minutes he heard the bird squawking and cursing – and then suddenly it went quiet. Bob was afraid he had actually harmed the parrot and he

quickly opened the freezer door. The parrot stepped out onto Bob's extended arm and said, "I'm sorry that I have offended you with my language and actions and I ask for your forgiveness. I will endeavor to correct my behavior." Bob was astonished at the bird's change in attitude and was about to ask what had caused such a drastic change when the parrot said: "Sir, may I ask what the chicken did?"

To the parrot, his change of behavior is based on a rational consideration – that Bob put the chicken in the freezer to punish him and that from the looks of it the chicken's offense was a lot greater than his own. Yet he makes an inferential mistake that is fundamentally irrational.

Here's another example:

A ventriloquist is doing a show in an out-of-the-way place and as part of his act he makes several jokes insulting the local residents. Finally a man in the audience who can't take it any more stands up. He shouts, "Hey! You on stage! You've been making fun of us all night! We ain't stupid, you know!" The ventriloquist responds, "Hey, relax, they're just jokes!" "I'm not talking to you," the man shouts back, "but to that little smart-ass sitting on your knee!"

Here the man in the audience makes a reasonable claim: "We ain't stupid, you know!" Unfortunately, he undermines his claim because he doesn't know how ventriloquism works. It may interest the reader to know that jokes about the low intelligence of other persons tend to support the theory held by Plato and Aristotle that humor derives from our feelings of superiority over other people or over ourselves at some earlier point in time. They may have been influenced by jokes about the stupidity of the Boeotians, the rustic peasant neighbors of Athens (Davies 1998, p. 11). Jokes about otherwise intelligent persons who say and do irrational things tend to support the theory held by Immanuel Kant and Arthur Schopenhauer that humor derives from situations where something occurs that clashes with what we would have expected in a particular set of circumstances. See Morreall (1987).

Finally, it's worth noting that despite the tendency of jokes to operate within a general content or framework of absurdity (see Cohen 1999, pp. 45–68), jokes actually depend on established standards of rationality. If there weren't such standards, and if jokes did not recognize that such standards exist, jokes that employ faulty reasoning would not be jokes. Their incongruous quality depends on the existence of such standards and the ability to "get" a joke often depends on one's ability to recognize how one or another of these standards is being violated by the joke.

Rationality and Acting Prudentially

The ability to distinguish between the rational and the irrational is an important aspect of critical thinking. Another is the ability to distinguish between the rational and the prudential. If acting rationally means that one is able to make use of practical reasoning in making decisions, choices, and the like, it makes a certain kind of sense to say that rational thinking tends to be prudential thinking, i.e., exercising sound judgment as far as desirable outcomes are concerned. In fact, there is a sense in which rational thinking may be defined or at least understood as prudential thinking. But this association of rational and prudential thinking raises certain questions in situations where there can be honest doubt or uncertainty as to what, in fact, is the most prudential decision or choice.

Here's an example:

> An angel appears at a faculty meeting and tells the dean that in return for his unselfish and exemplary behavior, the Lord will reward him with his choice of infinite wealth, wisdom, or beauty. Without hesitating, the dean selects infinite wisdom. "Done!" says the angel, and disappears in a cloud of smoke and a bolt of lightning. Now, all heads turn toward the dean, who sits surrounded by a faint halo of light. One of his colleagues whispers, "Say something." The dean sighs and says, "I should have taken the money."

The dean's decision to choose infinite wisdom was a rational one. After all, a major part of his job is to make wise decisions, so we can easily understand why he would have chosen infinite wisdom over infinite wealth and infinite beauty, and to have made this decision rather effortlessly. Viewed from the perspective of his position as dean, this decision was also a prudential one. Having infinite wisdom will make him a good and effective dean. Then, however, the very acquisition of infinite wisdom causes him to second-guess the decision: he should have opted instead for infinite wealth. From the perspective of his personal well-being, this probably would have been the more prudent thing to have chosen. Of course, one or another of his colleagues might choose to challenge this way of thinking: "The greatest philosophers in the history of humankind have chosen wisdom over wealth." On the other hand, this challenge would not get them very far because the dean could respond, "That's what I used to think before I received the gift of infinite wisdom." Most importantly for our purposes, the joke illustrates the fact that (1) we need to distinguish between the rational and the prudent because sometimes the most rational decision is *not* the most prudent; and (2) there may be circumstances in which prudential outcomes compete with one another. One thing we can probably all agree upon is that the dean would not have been acting rationally *or* prudently if he had chosen infinite beauty. In fact, the very imprudence of such a decision would be virtually tantamount to saying that his decision was irrational.

Having Good Reasons for What We Believe

Critical thinking involves having good reasons for what we believe. It also involves being able to tell if someone else has good reasons for what he or she believes. If good reasons for either are lacking, we may infer that the beliefs are irrational. The following joke is illustrative:

> A guy walks into a bar and asks, "Anyone know what time it is?" One of the patrons sitting at the end of the bar says, "Can't say for sure but I do know it ain't seven o'clock." "How do you know that?" " 'Cause I promised my wife I'd be home by then, and I ain't there."

Obviously, the second guy doesn't have a good reason to believe it's not seven o'clock. His belief is based on a faulty assumption. The faulty assumption is, "If it's seven o'clock then I must be home." What makes it faulty is that it is based on the guy's belief that he kept his promise to his wife. There may be circumstances when the same assumption would be valid, for example, when spoken by someone who obsessively follows a set schedule. As for the first guy, it would be irrational for him to believe the other guy. There's a chance that it isn't seven o'clock, but the other guy's grounds for believing it isn't seven o'clock are spurious and the first guy should recognize that this is the case.

Here's another example:

> An elderly woman was afraid to fly to visit her family because she was afraid that there would be a bomb on board. Her family tried to convince her that the risk was actually very small and to prove their point they persuaded her to consult an actuary. "What are the chances of there being a bomb on a plane?" she asked. "Very small," said the actuary, "about one in ten thousand." "And what are the chances of there being two bombs on a

plane?" "Even smaller" the actuary replied, "Something like one in a hundred million." So after that the elderly woman was happy to fly, as long, that is, as she brought a bomb on the plane with her.

Here the error in her thinking is the fact that by bringing her own bomb the elderly woman hasn't lessened the odds of there being another bomb on board: it is still 1 in 10,000.

Beliefs Have Practical Consequences

Like many of the previous jokes, these jokes about the guy in the bar who tells the other guy what time it is and the woman who carries a bomb onto the plane have practical implications. If the guy who asks what time it is actually believed the other guy, his belief in the reliability of the other guy's answer could have negative consequences. If the woman tries to bring a bomb on the plane, we can be quite sure that she will not be permitted to fly which would, of course, reduce the risks of flying to 0 percent but the odds of being placed in detention to 100 percent. So these jokes illustrate the fact that what we believe and our grounds for doing so have important practical implications. This is because our beliefs guide our actions, and if our beliefs are faulty then our actions are likely to be faulty as well. If we act on false or unsupported beliefs then our actions are less likely to achieve their goals. Here's an example:

> A wife tells her husband, "I think the baby is coming. We've got to get to the hospital. There's no time to lose!" Her husband leaps to his feet, goes to the door and as he runs out of the house he shouts to his wife, "It's rush hour and traffic's gonna be heavy. So let's take both cars so at least one of us will get there on time!"

While it may make sense to take two cars in some situations, as when a wife and husband plan to leave a party at different times, it's irrational to do so when the wife is in labor. It won't help if he gets there first because he is not the one who is having the baby, and if the baby begins to arrive while his wife is en route to the hospital, she will be in the impossible situation of driving and giving birth at the same time, and her husband won't be there to assist her. If the husband actually drives off without her, his irrational thinking could have disastrous consequences.

Similarly, immoral and unethical behavior is often the result of irrationality. Although it's true that some people act in ways that are self-consciously or deliberately immoral, most people act immorally because they fail to think critically. They may be ignorant of the consequences of their actions or they may not be aware of particular matters of fact; whatever the case, this ignorance or lack of awareness can lead to immoral actions. For these reasons, critical thinking can help persons avoid doing wrong to others, acting unjustly toward others, or engaging in actions that cause pain and suffering. If a person wants to do the right thing, this creates a strong incentive to be a critical thinker. Here's a joke that illustrates the connection between irrational thinking and doing the wrong thing:

> **Two hunters are out in the woods when one of them falls to the ground. He doesn't appear to be breathing and his eyes are rolled back in his head. The other hunter whips out his cell phone and calls 911. He gasps to the operator. "My friend is dead! What can I do!?" In a calm soothing voice, the operator replies, "Just take it easy. I can help. First, let's make sure that he's dead." There is silence then a shot is heard. The guy's voice comes back on the line. He says, "OK, now what?"**

In this example, the hunter makes a terrible mistake because he makes an inappropriate inference from what the operator says: there's the possibility that his friend is not dead and if that's the case, the operator's instructions will be different from the ones she will give if the friend is really dead. It's true that her wording – "Let's make sure that he's dead" – is ambiguous. This does not, however, excuse the fact that he wasn't thinking rationally. Some of us might want to give him the benefit of the doubt and say that he made this error in thinking because he had panicked. Even so, the joke illustrates that the failure to think rationally can result in immoral or unethical actions.

The Desire to Appear Intelligent to Others

Jokes illustrate another reason to be a critical thinker: Even as we generally do not want to act immorally or unethically, so we do not want to be shown to be misguided or wrong about whatever is being discussed. True, there are times when we enjoy looking stupid or being viewed by others as incredibly dumb; the enjoyment often comes from knowing that there are benefits from being viewed as dumb, such as the fact that we will not be expected to assume responsibility for solving the problem. So, being perceived as dumb can be the smart thing to do. But for the most part, we like others to think that we are smart and intelligent, and that our opinions have a lot to commend themselves. Many jokes, like the one about the hunter, play on our desire to appear intelligent by placing someone in a situation that calls for rational thinking but the person falls short. Take this example:

> A truck driver gets his truck stuck under a railroad bridge. He tries all sorts of things to get the truck unstuck, but nothing works. The top of the truck is wedged tightly against the bridge. Eventually a passerby comes up, looks at the truck, and suggests letting some air out of the tires. The truck driver stares angrily at him, "You moron! The truck is stuck on *top*!"

We find the truck driver amusing because he believes that he's the one who is thinking rationally when in fact the passerby is the one who offers a plausible solution to the truck driver's problem. Contrast the truck driver with the rabbi in the following joke:

> A minister, a priest, and a rabbi were out hiking. It was very hot, and they were tired and sweating when they came upon a small lake. Knowing it was fairly secluded, they decided to go skinny-dipping. They swam for a few minutes, and then, feeling refreshed, they decided to pick a few berries while enjoying their freedom. As they were crossing an open area, still naked, who should come along but a group of women from town? As they ran back into the wooded area, the minister and the priest covered their privates while the rabbi covered his face. As they were putting on their clothes, the minister and the priest asked the rabbi why he had covered his face instead of his privates. The rabbi replied, "I don't know about you, but in my congregation, it's my *face* they would recognize."

Here, the minister and the priest think the rabbi is acting irrationally but, in fact, his behavior in this rather dicey situation makes so much sense that he almost makes the minister and priest look irrational by comparison. In fact, his comment, "I don't know about you," seems an indirect way of saying that their behavior *was* irrational unless they had something else to hide. But the important point for our purposes here is that how we think has practical consequences, so it makes sense for us to want to become good critical thinkers, to have solid, rational grounds for what we believe and for what we do. Jokes can be helpful because they often illustrate how a person (or anthropomorphized bird or animal) thinks when confronted with a situation that calls for thinking. To be sure, the situations are rather contrived, but this very contrivance makes it easier to identify what makes the thinking fallacious or irrational.

In this chapter we have introduced several important features of critical thinking. One is the fact that the context plays an important role in thinking critically. Another is that critical thinking is based on established standards of rationality. A third is that critical thinking has important practical consequences because our beliefs have practical consequences and critical thinking involves having grounds for what we believe. A fourth is that critical thinking is a way to make ourselves appear intelligent to others. If having a high IQ does not guarantee that one thinks rationally, learning how to become a critical thinker levels the playing field. Like jokes, courses that teach critical thinking are democratic, not elitist. As the guy says to the ventriloquist, "We ain't all stupid, here." No, of course we're not. But some of us may give that impression:

> A student went to the college infirmary because he was suffering from constipation. The doctor prescribed suppositories. A week later he returned because the suppositories weren't having the desired results. "Have you been taking them regularly?" the doctor asked. "What do you think I've been doing," he replied, "shoving them up my butt?"

Good Point!

Voltaire said that heaven had given us two things to counterbalance
the many miseries of life, *hope* and *sleep*. He could have added
laughter, if the means of exciting it in reasonable persons were only
as easily attainable, and the requisite wit or originality of humor
were not so rare.

Immanuel Kant

Bad Limerick!!

An example of Kant's sterling wit
Was his theory that farts could be lit,
    And it's said that all night
    By the flickering light
He composed his *Critique of Pure Shit*.

Victor Gray

2 Fallacies of Relevance

Jokes are good ways of illustrating flawed reasoning. Here's an example, adapted from Sigmund Freud (1960, p. 69):

> A guy goes into a café, orders a pastry, and sits down. A few seconds later he brings the pastry back to the counter and asks to exchange it for a glass of liqueur. The proprietor agrees, the man goes back to his seat, slowly finishes his drink, and gets up to leave. "Hey," says the proprietor, "you can't leave until you pay for your drink." "But I exchanged my pastry for it." "You didn't pay for the pastry, either." "But I hadn't eaten it."

What's wrong with this reasoning? The customer's reasoning is flawed because it doesn't matter that he hadn't eaten his pastry. That fact, while true, does not support his claim that he is not obligated to pay for his drink. Instead, it's an irrelevant piece of information.

Such common errors in reasoning are called "fallacies." In this and the two following chapters we will cover a wide range of fallacies that, nevertheless, fall into three distinct categories. These categories are: (1) fallacies of relevance; (2) fallacies of evidence; and (3) fallacies of assumption. These categories, and the specific fallacies that fall within them, help us quickly identify the flaws in a piece of reasoning. They provide us with the conceptual tools that help us think critically about the reasons we give for a particular belief.

A few words of caution: First, our discussion of fallacies will be selective, not exhaustive. We won't discuss all the fallacies that are typically covered in critical thinking textbooks, but we will focus on the ones that occur most often or that have the most negative personal or social impact. Second, we don't assume that every example of bad reasoning can be neatly pigeon-holed as one fallacy or another and this is also true of jokes. A joke may illustrate more than one fallacy. On the other hand, jokes are not intended to illustrate the fallacies, so we expect that readers will sometimes disagree with our view that a joke illustrates a particular fallacy. We welcome these disagreements because they are evidence of the very fact that the reader is thinking critically, and that's why we went to the trouble to write this book. Third, different people will classify these fallacies differently. Some people classify the "post hoc" or "false cause" as a fallacy of relevance, others as a fallacy of evidence, and still others as a fallacy of assumption. We have reasons for our classification but we recognize that others may do it differently. Fourth, there's the danger of finding fallacies where none exist. Especially if one has fallacies on one's mind, it's rather easy to think a claim is fallacious when it really isn't. This often results from holding a person – or ourselves – to a standard of rationality that is too high given the situation. Since it is unreasonable to require everyone to be absolutely precise all of the time, it is usually better to treat a claim charitably than to denounce it as fallacious.

This chapter is about fallacies of relevance. A person commits a fallacy of relevance by giving an irrelevant reason in support of a belief. The joke we started with is an example. It's irrelevant that the customer hadn't eaten his pastry: he still owes for his drink.

We begin with fallacies of relevance because they are so fundamental to thinking critically. If someone's reasons are irrelevant then it doesn't matter if they are true or well supported. Thus, the first question to ask in determining whether someone has good reasons for what they believe is whether those reasons are relevant. If not, then there's no need to go any further.

Reasons are irrelevant in different ways and it is helpful to be aware of these differences. What follows are the most prominent fallacies of relevance.

Threat Disguised as Reason

One fallacy of relevance is one that uses a threat disguised as a reason. This is formally called the *ad baculum* fallacy because in Latin "baculum" means "the stick." Here's an example:

> **A guy suspects that his wife is cheating on him and, in a rage he goes out and buys a gun. The next day he comes home from work and finds his wife in bed with another man. Devastated, he pulls the gun out and points it at**

his own head. His wife says, "Honey! Don't do it! We can work this out!" "Shut up," he replies. "You're next."

Of course, the man's ability to commit homicide will be seriously hampered if he shoots himself first. But that's not our point here. The point is that he is using a threat while she is making an appeal to reason. We may be skeptical that they can "work this out," but his threat of violence does nothing to address the reasons she might have. It's entirely irrelevant. This is also true of the following version of the joke:

> Father O'Grady was greeting his parishioners after Sunday morning Mass when Mary Clancy came up to him in tears. "What is bothering you, my dear?" he inquired. "Oh, Father, I have terrible news. My husband passed away last night." "Oh, Mary, how terrible. Tell me, did he have any last requests?" "Well, yes, he did, Father. He said, 'Please, Mary, put down that gun … '"

It's pretty hard to appeal to reason when the other person is holding a loaded gun.

Here's a joke that illustrates the use of threat when one is unable to make an appeal based on reason and knows that this is the case:

> One day little Johnny asked his mother for a new bike. She replied, "At Christmas you send a letter to Santa to ask for what you want, don't you?" Johnny answered, "Yes, but Christmas is months away and I don't want to have to wait that long." She said, "Then why not send Jesus a letter and ask him?" Johnny sat down with a pen and paper and wrote, "Dear Jesus, I've been a good boy and I would like a new bike. Your friend, Johnny." He read it over and didn't like it, so he wrote another letter: "Dear Jesus, sometimes I'm a good boy and I would like a new bike. Your friend, Johnny." He didn't like this one either, so he wrote another letter: "Dear Jesus, I thought about being a good boy and I would like a new bike. Your friend, Johnny." He thought awhile and decided he didn't like this one either. He left and went walking around, depressed, when he passed by a house with a small statue of Mary in the front yard. He grabbed the statue and rushed home. He hid the statue under his bed, sat down again with pen and paper and wrote, "Dear Jesus, if you want to see your mother again, send me a new bike! Your friend, Johnny."

Johnny assumes he needs to make a case for why Jesus would give him a new bike and believes that it needs to be truthful because Jesus will know if it is not. Yet, the more truthful his appeal becomes, his case for a new bike gets weaker. Realizing his dilemma, he resorts to threat.

This is a fallacy of relevance because such threats are irrelevant to whether a particular claim is true. This highlights an important distinction: it's one thing to believe a claim because it is safe. Of course, what is true and what is safe often overlap, which is why this fallacy sometimes escapes notice. Many beliefs are safe but are not, for that reason, true. It may be safe, in a dictatorship, to believe everything the dictator says, but this doesn't make what he says true. Likewise, it may be prudent to believe that oysters are inedible (one can, after all, die from the bacteria in some oysters), but that doesn't make the belief itself true.

Another reason threats disguised as reasons are fallacious is that, although they may coerce behavior, they do not necessarily coerce belief. A person can use a threat to make another person act in a certain way, but this does not guarantee that the person will believe what the first person wants this person to believe. Knowing that a belief is safe or prudent doesn't make it any easier to believe. One may know that it's safe to agree with a dictator, but that doesn't necessarily make it any easier to believe. Even *wanting* to believe something doesn't make it any easier to believe. One may *want* to believe what a dictator says yet find it impossible to believe no matter how hard one tries. In fact, it seems to be a fact of human psychology that the more someone threatens us, the less likely we are to believe what they say, even if what they say is perfectly reasonable. If a parent threatens a child in order to coerce belief, the child is probably less, not more, likely to believe what the parent wants the child to believe, if only because the child can attribute his acquiescence to the parent's show of force.

This does not mean that threatening behavior is always wrong. Some situations may be serious enough to justify such a threat: for example, a coast guard ship might threaten to sink a boat if it fails to yield under certain circumstances. In such cases, where lives are at stake or a crime is being committed, a threat of force may be justified in order to prevent a greater wrong from taking place. In these cases, the threat is justified on the assumption that it helps achieve a beneficial outcome. However, threat does not, by itself, provide a reason for believing that a particular outcome is beneficial. The fact that one has a stick and is not afraid to use it is irrelevant as far as critical thinking is concerned. The following joke illustrates the point:

> **Four rabbis had a series of theological arguments and three were always in accord against the fourth. One day the odd rabbi out, after losing another argument by a vote of three to one, decided to appeal to a higher authority. "Oh, God!" he cried, "I know I am right and they are wrong. Please send a**

sign to prove it to them!" As soon as the rabbi finished his plea, a storm cloud moved across the sky and rain poured down on the four rabbis. "I knew I was right," the rabbi exulted, "the cloud and rain are a sign from God!" But the others disagreed, pointing out that storm clouds form on hot days. So he prayed again, "Oh, God, I need a bigger sign to show these skeptics that I'm right and they're wrong." This time a bolt of lightning slammed into a tree on a nearby hill. "I told you I was right!" the rabbi exclaimed, but the other three insisted that nothing had happened that could not be explained by natural causes. Just as the rabbi was about to ask for an even more impressive sign, a huge wind arose and it was so forceful that it slammed the three rabbis against a tree, leaving the lone rabbi standing. Then a streak of sunlight shone down on the rabbi and a voice declared, "You are right, my son." As he stood triumphantly over his stunned and quivering colleagues, the rabbi put his hands on his hips and said, "Well?" One of the other three replied, "So, now it's three to two."

The three rabbis have been rather severely threatened, and the fact that God is the agent of the threat would suggest that it would be prudent for the three rabbis to acquiesce, but they refuse to be cowed by the fact that God has a very large stick.

Appeal to Inappropriate Authority

A second fallacy of relevance is the appeal to an inappropriate authority in support of one's belief or truth claim. Formally, this is known as the "*ad verecundiam*" fallacy because in Latin "verecundiam" means "authority." There's nothing wrong with relying on expert testimony or the voice of authority. Since we can't know everything, or be everywhere at once, we need to rely on experts on a variety of issues. This only works, though, when the authorities are appropriate, when, for example, we ask chemists about chemistry, lawyers about the legal system, mechanics about auto repair, etc. When we appeal to testimony by people who are speaking from outside their area of expertise or who, for one reason or another, do not really know what they are talking about, we commit an appeal to inappropriate authority. Here's an example:

A lawyer, an engineer, and computer programmer are in a car, driving in the mountains. The engineer is driving. They're driving downhill, and as they come up on a sharp curve, he pushes the brake pedal and feels it sink smoothly all the way to the floor. He holds on and manages to get the car around the curve. He pulls on the emergency brake handle and it comes off in his hand. He sees a hairpin curve above a high falloff straight ahead and knows that he'll never be able to pull the car around that curve. In a last-ditch effort, he yanks the wheel sideways, puts the car in a sideways skid, and brings it to a stop just inches from the edge. Everyone takes a deep breath, and gets out. The lawyer starts panicking. "We could have been killed! These defective brake systems constitute a tort against us. We should sue!" The engineer calms him down, and suggests that they pop open the hood to see if they can figure out what happened, and see if they can fix it. The computer programmer says, "I think you're both overreacting. Before we do either of those things, let's push the car back up the mountain and see if it happens again."

Each of the occupants of the car appeals to his own area of expertise. The lawyer's comment, although true enough, is not especially helpful at the moment. The computer programmer's proposal, although appropriate for a computer, is irrelevant in this case because a car and a computer are very different machines. Following his advice could have very negative consequences. Thus, in this situation, we would want to take the advice of the engineer because he makes the most reasonable proposal. Maybe they'll be able to figure out what went wrong and fix the problem. Even if they can't, it makes sense to try this approach instead of the one the computer programmer suggests. Of course, our preference for the engineer's proposal doesn't undercut the lawyer's authority when it comes to what they might do in the aftermath of this near disaster. Nor should we necessarily conclude that the computer programmer's rather poor judgment in this case should influence our views about his ability to solve computer-related problems: it just means that there are situations where a mediocre mechanic may be a better authority than an outstanding programmer.

Here's another example:

A young man had just acquired his learner's permit and wanted to borrow the family car. His father says, "I'll make a deal with you. I'll let you borrow the car if you keep your grades up, study your Bible, and cut your hair." A month later the son comes back and says, "Dad, I'm doing great in all my classes and reading the Bible every night. Can I borrow the car?" "But you haven't cut your hair," his father replies. The son pauses for a moment, "I've been thinking about this and Noah had long hair and so did Moses, Samson, David, and Absalom. Even Jesus had long hair." His father answered, "You're right. And they walked everywhere they went."

There are a couple of issues here. One has to do with the son and father's specific claims: that the four biblical characters had long hair and that they walked everywhere they went. Of the four mentioned, the only one where there is evidence that he had long hair is Samson because an issue is made of the fact that Delilah had a Philistine cut off the seven locks of his hair (Judges 16:19). (Absalom is typically considered to have had long hair because he got caught in a tree, but the text [2 Samuel 18:9] merely says that his head got caught in the tree.) The story about a large group of small boys making fun of Elisha because he was baldheaded (2 Kings 2:23–5) may suggest that long hair was the norm, but the son has no solid proof that all of these biblical characters had long hair.

The father's claim that they walked everywhere they went is even more questionable. After all, Absalom was riding a mule when his head got caught in a tree, Jesus rode a donkey into Jerusalem, and Noah had an ark that enabled him to ride out the flood. The son could also have responded that people rode camels and horses in those days. It's obviously true that they didn't ride around in automobiles, but that's beside the point.

Another issue, however, has to do with the very appeal that son and father both make to the Bible. The father had stipulated that his son could borrow the family car if he got good grades, read the Bible every night, and cut his hair. The son accepted these stipulations and has met two of them but not all three. His appeal to the Bible in support of his unwillingness to meet the third stipulation is simply an appeal to an inappropriate authority. After all, what biblical characters did or did not do is irrelevant to the agreement that the son and father had made in regard to the son's use of the family car. Conceivably, the son could produce an appropriate authority who would support his unwillingness to cut his hair, although it is difficult to imagine what authority this might be, but, in any case, he has not done so. The Bible may be an appropriate authority in other instances, but the son has not provided any reasons why it should be viewed as such in this instance, and the father should simply have pointed this out rather than attempting to provide counter-evidence derived from this alleged authority.

Often, we commit this fallacy because we assume that someone who is an expert in one field will be an expert in another. And, to a certain extent, that may be true. We can reasonably expect that a patent lawyer, say, will know a thing or two about contract law (or at least will know a lot more about it than a non-lawyer). Or a person may be an expert in two unrelated areas: English literature and home renovation, for example. Also, there are a few individuals who seem to know a lot about an awful lot of things. But we need to keep in mind that expertise doesn't *necessarily* transfer from one field to another, and there are plenty of people who are experts in one field and completely incompetent outside it.

Conversely, just because someone is incompetent in one field doesn't mean that his or her claim to be competent in another is false. Consider this joke:

> A guy goes into a bar, approaches the bartender, and says, "I've been working on a top secret project on molecular genetics for the past five years and I've just got to talk to someone about it." The bartender says, "Wait a minute. Before we talk about that, just answer a couple of questions. When a deer defecates, why does it come out like little pellets?" The guy doesn't know. The bartender then asks, "Why is it that when a dog poops, it lands on the ground and looks like a coiled rope?" The guy, again, says, "I don't have any idea." The bartender then says, "You don't know crap and you want to talk about molecular genetics?"

No doubt, the bartender doesn't want to get into a discussion of molecular genetics, so he challenges the other guy on his knowledge of "crap." But just because the other guy doesn't know "crap" does not mean that he isn't an authority on molecular genetics. The two areas of expertise have nothing to do with one another.

In general, the appeal to inappropriate fallacy reminds us that the *reasons* behind a claim matter more than the *person* making the claim. In fact, what makes a person an expert is the ability to give reasons for what he or she claims. That's what distinguishes expert opinion from a mere lucky guess. Thus, even when we must rely on expert testimony, merely being an expert on something or other is not enough. That someone is an expert is irrelevant unless the topic falls under their area of expertise. Many jokes about professionals play on this basic rule of rational argument. They poke fun at a profession's expertise by placing it out of context. Here's a joke about doctors:

> Three doctors are out hunting ducks and a bird flies overhead. The general practitioner looks at it and says, "Looks like a duck, flies like a duck … It must be a duck." He shoots at it and misses, and the bird flies away. The next bird flies overhead, and the pathologist looks at it, then skims through the pages of a bird manual, and says, "Hmmm … Green wings, yellow bill, quacking sound … It must be a duck." He raises his gun to shoot it, but the bird has already flown away. A third bird flies over. The surgeon raises his gun and shoots almost without looking, brings the bird down, and turns to the pathologist and says, "Go see if that was a duck."

These doctors may be very good in their medical specialties, but the qualities that make them good physicians may be exactly what make them poor duck hunters. For example, we may prefer a surgeon who has an aggressive, shoot-first-and-ask-questions-later attitude if we want someone to remove a cancerous growth. On the other hand, we don't want someone with a shoot-first-and-ask-questions-later attitude when hunting ducks, especially if there are other humans around. Here's a final example:

> An accountant is visiting a natural history museum and looking at a dinosaur skeleton. "You know," he says to his neighbor, "that dinosaur is 75 million 6 months old." "How can you be so precise?" "Well," the accountant replies, "the last time I was there the guide said it was 75 million years old, and that was 6 months ago."

Once again, such precision may be necessary when balancing the books, but one shouldn't confuse an accountant's authority for that of a paleontologist.

Appeal to the Public

A third fallacy of relevance is the claim that something is true and/or worth believing because it is widely believed to be true. This is formally called the *"ad populum"* fallacy because in Latin "populum" means "the public." We all know – or like to think we know – that the fact something is widely held to be true does not necessarily mean that it is true; nor does the fact that something is widely done necessarily mean that it makes sense to do it. Just because other people believe or do a certain thing it doesn't follow that we all should (or that you should). In nearly all cases the fact that a belief is widely held is irrelevant to whether that belief is true (we'll discuss an exception shortly). Consider this joke:

> A father enters the bathroom to brush his teeth and finds that his son, Billy, is already there. The father says in a stern and exasperated voice, "Billy, how many times do I have to tell you not to play with that thing. If you keep doing that, you could go blind." Billy responds, "Hey, Dad, I'm over here."

There was a time when many people – probably the majority – believed that masturbation causes blindness (Trevor-Roper 1988, pp. 155–6). It was also widely believed that it causes mental illness (Skultans 1975, pp. 57–62, 86–94). Obviously, the fact that people believed these things about masturbation does not make it true.

Critical thinking does not only involve beliefs. It also involves actions. The appeal to the fact that others are doing it can be just as problematic as appealing to the fact that others believe it. Here's a joke that illustrates why it's a good idea to think critically about what others are doing and their reasons for doing so before you follow their example:

> On a train to a conference dealing with medical malpractice, there were a bunch of lawyers and a bunch of doctors. Each of the doctors had a train ticket, but the lawyers had only one ticket between them. The doctors laughed, thinking that the lawyers would get thrown off the train. When one of the lawyers, the lookout, said, "Here comes the conductor," all of the lawyers went into the bathroom. The doctors were puzzled. The conductor came along and said, "Tickets, please," taking tickets from each of the doctors. He then knocked on the bathroom door and said, "Ticket, please." The lawyers slid their one ticket under the door. The conductor took it and moved on. The doctors felt foolish for not realizing what the lawyers were up to. So, on the way back from the conference, the doctors decided they would try the same gambit. They bought one ticket for the whole group. Then they met up with the lawyers who were on the same train. Again, the doctors snickered at the lawyers but this time *none* of the lawyers had tickets. When the lookout said, "Conductor coming!" all the lawyers went to one bathroom and all the doctors went to the other bathroom. Before the conductor entered the car, one of the lawyers left their bathroom, knocked on the doctors' bathroom and said, "Ticket, please."

We can imagine what went through the doctors' heads: "All those lawyers rode for free! We should ride for free, too." If that's what they thought, then they committed the fallacy of the appeal to the fact that other people are doing it. The mere fact that the lawyers ride for free is no reason for the doctors to think that they either can or should do the same. As it happens, the joke makes this point clear: the doctors were foolish to believe they could steal the lawyers' trick, and, of course, they were wrong to try to do so.

It's not hard to see why appealing to the popularity of a belief or behavior is a fallacy, specifically, a fallacy of relevance. After all, there are many historical examples of how the majority can be mistaken. As noted above, people have held false views about the effects of masturbation. On the other hand, it can sometimes be difficult to distinguish between valid and invalid appeals to what is widely held or believed. For example, if a man has the type of color-blindness called deuteranomaly (and about 6% of men do) then he will have trouble distinguishing black objects from dark green objects. If he is unsure whether he has grabbed his black sweater or his dark green sweater and it matters to him to choose the right one, it makes sense to ask other people for their judgment. If they all tell him that the sweater he has grabbed is black, then this is what he should believe. Furthermore, he shouldn't ask just one person because this person could also have the same type of color-blindness; by asking more people, he reduces the likelihood that this would be the case.

But why is this not an example of the fallacy? It's basically because the vast majority of people are pretty good at distinguishing black from dark green. If the question were more technical and specialized, such as matching the exact color for restoring Leonardo da Vinci's *The Last Supper*, then we'd be negligent if we merely trusted the general public. In such cases a more expert opinion is called for. In a sense, therefore, this fallacy is a kind of appeal to inappropriate authority where the inappropriate authority is the general public (or a major segment of it). So, just as some appeals to authority are valid, sometimes there is no problem in appealing to what is generally believed. On the other hand, it is never the public's judgment in and of itself that gives support to a claim. Rather, it's the underlying reasons for its beliefs that matter.

Targeting the Person

A fourth fallacy of relevance involves targeting the person and ignoring the reasons the person gives for a belief or action. This is formally called the "*ad hominem*" fallacy because in Latin "hominem" means "the man" or "the person." This fallacy is the flip side of the appeal to inappropriate authority fallacy. While the inappropriate authority fallacy appeals to who a person is in order to *accept* a belief or act in a certain way, this fallacy appeals to who a person is in order to *reject* a belief or action. It, too, is a fallacy of relevance because what matters are the reasons and evidence that support the belief.

Many of the jokes that illustrate this fallacy are about lawyers. The assumption is that if a lawyer says it, it can't possibly be true. Here's a joke that illustrates the general idea:

> A young boy asked his lawyer father, "Dad, does a lawyer ever tell the truth?" The father thought for a moment, "Yes, son. Sometimes a lawyer will do anything to win a case."

Here's a joke that provides a concrete illustration of why you can't believe whatever a lawyer claims to be true:

> A lawyer was on vacation in a small farming town. While walking through the streets on a quiet Sunday morning, he came upon a large crowd gathered by the side of the road. Going by instinct, the lawyer figured that there was some sort of auto collision. He was eager to get to the injured parties, but couldn't get near the car. Being a clever sort, he started shouted loudly, "Let me through! Let me through! I am the son of the victim." The crowd made way for him. Lying in front of the car was a donkey.

Psychiatrists also come in for quite a lot of ribbing in jokes. Here's an example:

> A guy goes into a psychiatrist's office and says that he is George Washington. He finishes up the session by telling the psychiatrist, "Tomorrow we will cross the Delaware and surprise them when they least expect it." As soon as the guy leaves the room, the psychiatrist picks up the phone and says, "King George, this is Benedict Arnold. I have the plans."

Old people are also targeted in jokes.

> Sitting on the side of the highway waiting to catch speeding drivers, a state trooper sees a car puttering along at twenty-two miles per hour. He thinks to himself, "This driver is just as dangerous as a speeder!" So he turns on his flashing lights and pulls the driver over. Approaching the car, he notices that there are five old ladies – two in the front seat and three in the back – wide-eyed and white as ghosts. The driver, confused, says to him, "Officer, I don't understand. I was doing exactly the speed limit! What seems to be the problem?" "Ma'am," the officer replies, "you weren't speeding, but you should know that driving slower than the speed limit can also be a danger to other drivers." "What do you mean, slower than the speed limit? No sir, I was doing the speed limit exactly – 22 miles an hour!" the old woman proudly replies. The officer explains to her that 22 was the route number, not the speed limit. A bit embarrassed, the woman grins and thanks the officer for pointing out the error. "Before I let you go, ma'am, I have to ask: Is everyone in this car okay? These women seem awfully shaken, and they

haven't muttered a single peep this whole time." "Oh, they'll be all right in a minute, officer. We just got off Route 119."

These three jokes play on common stereotypes of the three groups: lawyers put self-interest above upholding the law, psychiatrists are crazier than the people they treat, and elderly people are terrible drivers.

We aren't concerned here with whether these stereotypes may or may not have a grain of truth. Instead, what interests us is the fact that the lawyer, psychiatrist, and elderly woman are presented in these jokes as unreliable, i.e., you would be a fool to believe what they believe to be the case. Thus, these jokes illustrate how the *ad hominem* fallacy works: You identify the person as a "lawyer," a "psychiatrist," an "old lady," and the fallacy takes it from there.

Another type of *ad hominem* joke focuses on certain ethnic groups. Some of these are offensive and violate the standards of civility that are central to critical thinking. Being able to differentiate between jokes that violate these standards and jokes that do not is itself, in fact, a test of our critical reasoning skills. We tend to think that jokes that Norwegians and Swedes tell on one another do not violate these standards because they tell the same jokes and merely change the nationality of the person or persons in the joke. Here's an example:

Anders came home from school and asked his mother, "Mom, why am I the biggest boy in the second grade? Is it because I'm Swedish?" His mother replied, "No, my boy, it's because you're 17 years old."

The 17-year-old boy could just as well have been a Norwegian. Here's another example:

To avoid the livestock tax levied at the border between Norway and Sweden, a couple of Norwegian farmers dressed a hog in overalls and placed him between them in the front seat of their pickup truck as they crossed the border into Sweden. The Swedish border guard eyed the trio, asking their names. "Ole Johnson." "Lars Johnson." Then the hog: "Oink." Passing them on, the guard remarked to his assistant, "I've seen some awful looking people in my time, but that Oink Johnson has got to be the ugliest Norwegian I've ever laid eyes on!"

Here the Norwegian farmers outsmart the Swedish guard and save themselves the livestock tax. The Swedish guard looks foolish and the Norwegian farmers come off looking smart and clever. On the other hand, they outsmart the guard by passing the hog off as one of them, which doesn't reflect a very flattering self-image. Of course, they could just as easily have been Swedish farmers pulling a fast one on a Norwegian border guard.

Another example of the targeting of the person is self-directed or self-deprecating humor. For example, Rodney Dangerfield tells this joke on himself: "I told my psychiatrist that everyone hates me, but my psychiatrist replied, 'That's not true. Not everyone has met you yet.'" Making oneself the target of a joke can be a useful way for us to discourage other people from engaging in *ad hominem* attacks against us. This joke is an especially good illustration of the *ad hominem* fallacy, though, because the psychiatrist rejects Dangerfield's claim – "Everyone hates me" – on personal grounds: "That's not true. Not everyone has met you yet."

In general, we shouldn't reject a claim simply because of who makes it. A person's sex, race, ethnicity, age, sexual orientation, etc., are irrelevant to whether they speak the truth or have good reasons for what they say. *Who* they are is irrelevant to the *truth* of what they say. Unfortunately, we all too often judge a message based on the messenger. For example, there is evidence that juries find witnesses of certain ethnicities less believable than others (Lindholm 2005). One's ethnicity is irrelevant to one's credibility, yet it seems to affect people's perceptions.

However, there are some situations where one's identity is relevant in judging the truth of what one says. For example, while one's ethnicity is irrelevant to one's credibility, being a pathological liar is very relevant. One would not commit the *ad hominem* fallacy to disbelieve a statement made by a pathological liar. After all, this piece of information gives us good reason to question what the person says because it is directly relevant to its credibility. In a family counseling case, the father had this to say in response to the therapist's query as to what he considered the main problems in the family: "My contribution to our problem is that I'm a habitual liar. A lot of people will use the expression falsehood or exaggeration or bull-slinger, many things – but actually it's lying" (Watzlawick 1967, pp. 197–8). On the one hand, it should prove helpful to the therapist to know that the father is a self-professed habitual liar. On the other hand, this very fact is likely to complicate therapy with the family because his habit of lying will cast reasonable doubt on what he says or claims during the therapy sessions.

Thus, it is appropriate to doubt the claims that some persons make if there is reason to believe that they lack expertise on the matter in question, if they are mentally impaired, and so forth. On the other hand, even when a person's identity is relevant, we must be careful not to reject this person's statement or claim merely because of this. The fact that a person is a tobacco lobbyist should not, by itself, lead us to reject his claim that second-hand smoke is not the serious problem others have made it out to be. But it should make us more cautious, and lead us to scrutinize his claim more closely. Where there are clear conflicts of interest it would be naïve not to do so. Critical thinking is about the reasons we give for what we believe and do. Because *ad hominem* arguments focus on the persons and not on their reasons, they are an unnecessary and inappropriate distraction from what is really at issue.

Accusing a Person of Hypocrisy

A fifth fallacy of relevance occurs when we accuse someone of hypocrisy, i.e., of an inconsistency between what the person claims to believe or advocate and what the person actually does. Formally, this is called the *tu quoque* fallacy because "tu quoque" is Latin for "you, too." If Steve tells Jack that he should quit smoking cigarettes because they are highly addictive, carcinogenic, smelly, and expensive, and Jack replies that Steve is a fine one to talk because he is a three-pack-a-day smoker, Jack has committed this fallacy of relevance by attacking Steve's character (the inconsistency between what he advises and what he does himself) and not the reasons for his belief. This fallacy may therefore be viewed as a version of the *ad hominem* fallacy because it focuses on the person rather than on the reasons given for a belief. If Jack wanted to challenge Steve's reasons for quitting smoking, he might note that one of the reasons Steve gives – that smoking is addictive – makes the other reasons, although true, also moot.

Here's a joke which illustrates the fact that this is a fallacy of relevance:

> **A psychiatrist who is seeing a patient for the first time gives him the Rorschach ink blot test. He shows the patient the first card and asks what he sees. He looks at the card and blurts out, "A couple making love!" The psychiatrist shows the patient the second card. He looks at it and says, "A couple making love!" This goes on for every card. Finally, the psychiatrist says, "I think I know what your problem is. You're obsessed with sex." The patient replies, "Me? You're the one showing the dirty pictures!"**

Here the patient dismisses the psychiatrist's diagnosis by accusing him of having the same obsession. But that's irrelevant: even if the psychiatrist did have the same obsession this wouldn't necessarily undermine his diagnosis. After all, we trust doctors to make diagnoses even though they may suffer from the same diseases. In fact, we might trust the diagnosis even more, especially if we keep in mind the difference between a diagnosis and a cure. The patient's implied accusation – "You're the one showing the dirty pictures" – is a distraction from the real issue, which is that the man has consulted the psychiatrist and has sought a diagnosis, but when the diagnosis is presented, he changes the subject. Of course, the psychiatrist's diagnosis may be incorrect. If so, the patient should give reasons for why he thinks it is incorrect and/or ask the psychiatrist to provide more convincing reasons for why *he* believes this is probably the correct diagnosis.

Although this fallacy is most clearly associated with the *ad hominem* fallacy, there is also a sense in which it is related to the appeal to the larger public fallacy, only in reverse. Where the appeal to the larger public fallacy says, in effect, that it must be true because others do it, this one seeks to take the focus off oneself by implicating the other person – "you do it too." The following joke is illustrative:

> **"You are a cheat!" shouted the attorney to his opponent. "And you are a liar!" bellowed the opposition. Banging his gavel sharply, the judge interrupted: "All right, all right. Now that both attorneys have been identified, let's get on with this case."**

In effect, the judge agrees with both lawyers' assessments of one another. This joke illustrates the fact, however, that when one accuses the other, one tends to take the pressure off oneself.

Finally, it's worth emphasizing that the "you too" fallacy involves an *unfair* accusation of hypocrisy. But there are times when such an accusation *is* fair and should make us question what we've been told. This is especially true when someone can gain from being hypocritical. In the joke about the psychiatrist, the patient's implied charge of hypocrisy might be countered by noting that the psychiatrist would not have anything to gain from deliberately showing him "dirty pictures." However, in the following joke the grounds for claiming hypocrisy are much more self-evident. In fact, the perpetrator incriminates oneself:

> **Randi walked into a post office one day to see a middle-aged, balding man standing at the counter methodically placing "Love" stamps on bright pink**

envelopes with hearts all over them. He then took out a perfume bottle and started spraying scent all over each envelope. Randi's curiosity getting the better of her, she went up to the man and asked him what he was doing. The man said, "I'm sending out five hundred Valentine cards signed 'Guess who?'" "But why?" she asked. "I'm a divorce lawyer," he replied.

In short, hypocrisy is a fact of life. It's when we use this fact as a substitute for examining the grounds for the other person's assertion that we commit this fallacy. In effect, a person who commits this fallacy gives an irrelevant reason to reject a particular claim. And, like all *ad hominem* fallacies, what makes the reason irrelevant is that it focuses on the person making the claim rather than on the merits of the claim itself.

The Appeal to Pity

A sixth fallacy of relevance is the appeal to pity. In effect, one's claim is based on an emotional appeal. To call this a fallacy is not to critique pity as a fundamental human emotion. Rather, it is to say that, where critical thinking is concerned, pity is not an appropriate basis for assessing a person's claim. Consider this joke:

A lawyer appealed to the judge to have mercy on his client, a young man who had murdered his father and mother: "May I remind you, your honor, that this poor fellow is an orphan."

In effect, the lawyer asks the judge to take pity on the defendant when he sentences him. The fact that his client murdered his parents is not in dispute, but the lawyer wants to make an issue of the fact that this makes his client a de facto orphan. Of course, he conveniently overlooks or seeks to minimize the fact that the defendant is the reason he's an orphan. The lawyer commits a fallacy of relevance because the fact that his client is an orphan is irrelevant to the sentencing of the defendant. Other facts may be relevant. This one is not.

Appeals to pity are attempts to pull at our heartstrings. The lawyer uses the word "orphan" because it conjures up mental images of children who are bereft of both parents due to circumstances that are beyond their control (their parents have died, have abandoned them, and so forth). His use of the word certainly stretches its ordinary connotations and the mental images it evokes. Most importantly, just because we feel sorry for someone doesn't mean that we should either believe what they say or do as they ask. For example, parents who lose a child in an auto accident may want to blame the car manufacturer. Even though our hearts do go out to them we shouldn't conclude that the car maker is to blame *merely* because we sympathize with the parents. In other words, the fact that someone is pitiable is not a reason to believe what they say to be true.

However, some care is called for here. We shouldn't confuse a fallacious appeal to pity with valid mitigating circumstances. If a man steals a loaf of bread to feed his hungry family we will, of course, feel pity for the man that his family is hungry. We will also treat him more leniently because a hungry family would justify breaking the law, at least in some circumstances. In other words, his hungry family is a mitigating circumstance. The critical difference between this case and that of the young man who murdered his parents is that the hungry family is a reason to steal while the man's being an orphan is not a reason for the judge to exercise leniency.

To take a real-life example, consider the case of Andrea Yates, who drowned her five children in Houston, Texas, in 2001. In the two years prior to the murders, Yates had been diagnosed with postpartum depression and psychosis, had attempted suicide twice, and was twice committed to a psychiatric hospital. In the weeks before her murders, her doctor had also changed her medications. In the first murder trial, the prosecution argued that she should receive the death penalty. Her lawyers argued that because she suffered from postpartum depression and psychosis she deserved treatment more than punishment. In that first trial the jury found her guilty but refused to sentence her to death, instead sentencing her to forty years in prison. After that sentence was overturned (because a prosecution witness had lied), a second jury found her not guilty by reason of insanity (she believed that Satan had commanded her to drown her children) and she was committed indefinitely to a state psychiatric hospital. There can be no doubt that Andrea Yates' actions were horrific. However, given her psychiatric diagnosis, and the failure of others to give her adequate care, most people would conclude that she should not be treated the same as a typical mass murderer or serial killer (who very well may deserve to be executed). In addition, this conclusion does not depend on an appeal to pity because the fact that Yates was psychotic is relevant in determining how much punishment she deserves or is warranted.

Contrast Yates' case with that of Jason McCarthy, an Ohio man who was accused of trying to sell his two-year-old son in order to buy drugs.

During his trial McCarthy said, "I'm pretty tore up, and I want to get my son back. I got a month in jail and I lost my son and that's enough" (Engle 2007). McCarthy makes a common appeal to pity: hasn't he "suffered enough"? Most people would probably respond, "No, he hasn't suffered enough." His feelings of remorse, his month in jail, and the loss of the son whom he had been willing to sell, are not enough to make up for his crime. In fact, they fall so far short of making up for his crime that they are practically irrelevant. Although some people may pity or be sympathetic to Mr. McCarthy's expression of self-pity, this, by itself, is not a reason to treat him more leniently. As we noted in chapter 1, critical thinking is based on established standards of rationality, and generally connotes the absence of emotionality. This is not because emotions are considered inherently inferior or deceptive but because critical thinking is, by definition, the ability to reason, especially by drawing conclusions from evidence.

Finally, we should note that in our comments on these two cases, we said that "most people" would conclude that Yates ought not be treated the same as a mass murderer or serial killer and that "most people" would conclude that McCarthy has not suffered enough. To make these observations is not to commit the "appeal to the public" fallacy because they are not based on majority opinion *per se* but on the reasoning behind these conclusions.

The Appeal to Ignorance

A seventh fallacy of relevance is the appeal to ignorance. Formally, it is called the *ad ignorantiam* fallacy because in Latin "ad ignorantiam" means "ignorance." This fallacy involves confusing the absence of evidence with the presence of evidence. Typically, it confuses the absence of evidence *against* a claim with the presence of evidence *for* a claim. Conversely, an appeal to ignorance can also involve confusing the absence of evidence *for* a claim with the presence of evidence *against* a claim. For the sake of simplicity, we will focus only on the first version. In this case, an appeal is made to one's state of ignorance, and this state of ignorance is taken to be evidence in support of a particular belief. This is a fallacy of relevance because, in many cases, one's ignorance is irrelevant to the truth or falsity of a claim.

Here's a children's joke that illustrates an appeal to ignorance:

"Why do elephants paint their toenails red?" "I don't know." "So they can hide in cherry trees." "But I've never seen an elephant in a cherry tree!" "See! It works!"

This is an appeal to ignorance because it takes the absence of evidence *against* a claim (no one's ever caught sight of an elephant in a cherry tree) to be evidence *for* the claim (that elephants hide in cherry trees by painting their toenails red). But, obviously, we should require more evidence in support of the claim that elephants do this. For example, we might ask for evidence that elephants *do* frequent cherry trees or that they *do* in fact paint their toenails. Without such positive evidence, it doesn't matter much that no one has caught sight of an elephant hiding in a cherry tree. Given the absurdity of this claim, the burden is on the claimant to provide some positive evidence that elephants hide in cherry trees and not just point to the absence of evidence as "proof" that they are so well hidden that no one has ever seen one there. One's ignorance has no bearing on whether this claim is true: it is irrelevant that one is ignorant of evidence against this claim.

Here's another example:

A psychiatrist was escorting a patient from one psychiatric hospital to another. They were traveling by train, and the psychiatrist was intrigued to see the patient tearing up bits of paper and throwing them out the window. "What are you doing that for?" asked the psychiatrist. "To keep the tigers away," the patient replied. "But there are no tigers in New Jersey," the psychiatrist pointed out. "Effective, isn't it?" the patient answered.

Here, too, the patient commits an appeal to ignorance. He claims that tearing up bits of paper keeps tigers away. He then takes the fact that there's no evidence *against* this claim (who would check?) as evidence in *support* of the claim. But the fact that there are no tigers in New Jersey does not support the claim that tearing up bits of paper and throwing them away keeps the tigers away. Again, this claim is so absurd that it requires positive evidence on its behalf, not just the absence of counter evidence. The fact that we're ignorant of evidence against this claim is irrelevant. (This joke can also be taken as an example of the false cause or *post hoc* fallacy which we discuss in the next chapter.)

Whether a claim is an appeal to ignorance often depends on where the burden of proof lies. As a result, some claims may look like appeals to ignorance even though they really aren't. Depending on the claim, the absence of counterevidence may, in fact, be good reason to accept that claim. For example, since no one has disproved the theory of plate tectonics (which explains geological phenomena in terms of the movement of the earth's plates), it is rational to believe it.

This isn't an appeal to ignorance for two reasons. The first reason is that in making this claim we are implicitly relying on the well-supported belief that scientific theories undergo a lot of scrutiny. Therefore, it is safe to assume that if the theory of plate tectonics is false, then this would have been shown. That it hasn't been disproved is therefore a point in its favor. The second reason this isn't an appeal to ignorance is because of everything else we know about plate tectonics. In making the above claim we're also implicitly relying on all the good evidence in support of the theory. The absence of counter evidence, when combined with the presence of good evidence, increases the likelihood that the theory of plate tectonics is true.

There is one other situation when a claim might *look* like an appeal to ignorance but really isn't. Take this example: Because the prosecution did not prove Tony Soprano was a racketeer, he was not guilty of being a racketeer. Because of how the United States justice system works, this isn't an appeal to ignorance. In this system the burden of proof is on the prosecution, so "not guilty" does not mean the same as "innocent." Therefore, from the fact that the prosecution did not prove their case it *does* mean, as a matter of law, that Soprano is not guilty. It doesn't mean that he was therefore innocent.

As these examples show, whether a claim is an appeal to ignorance depends partly on where the burden of proof lies. If the burden of proof is on the person *making* a claim, then it isn't enough to point to the absence of counter evidence. The reason there is no counter evidence may simply be because no one has bothered to look. If, instead, the burden of proof is on the person who *questions* a claim, then pointing to the absence of counter evidence can be appropriate. That's because we would expect a person who questions a claim to cite some evidence for doing so. If they can't do this, then we're justified in ignoring their claim. Unfortunately, it's sometimes difficult to tell where exactly the burden of proof lies, and this itself can be a contentious issue.

Many jokes play on the idea that the true identity of the father of a child may be unknown. In effect, they warn us about the negative consequences of not knowing who the real father is. Here's an example:

> A married couple went to the hospital to have their baby delivered. Upon their arrival, the doctor said he had invented a new machine that would transfer a portion of the mother's labor pain to the father. He asked if they were willing to try it out. They were both very much in favor of it. The doctor set the knob to 10 percent for starters, explaining that even 10 percent was probably more pain than the father had ever experienced before. But as the labor progressed, the husband felt fine, so he asked the doctor to go ahead and bump it up a notch. He raised it to 20 percent, then 50 percent. The husband said he was feeling fine, so well, in fact, that he encouraged the doctor to transfer all the pain to him. The wife delivered a healthy baby with virtually no pain. She and her husband were ecstatic. But when they got home, they found the mailman dead on their porch.

This joke does not illustrate the fallacy of the appeal to ignorance. After all, the husband does not say that because he doesn't know the true identity of the father the father must be him. However, it does support our point in chapter 1 that critical thinking has practical consequences, and that these consequences are likely to be better than if one does not engage in critical thinking. The joke suggests that someone should have been suspicious when although the pain was transferred to the husband he didn't feel any of it. It did not occur either to the husband or to the doctor that maybe there was a flaw in their thinking, namely, their assumption that he was the father.

Here's a joke that plays on the idea that someone may be ignorant of how babies are actually conceived:

> Ole and Lena stood up for the wedding of Lars and Helga. Shortly after the wedding, the newlyweds moved away and Ole and Lena didn't see their friends for six years. Then, when the two couples got together again, Lars and Helga showed off their five children. Helga was very proud of her children. As they watched the children play together, Helga confided to Lena, "It sure was lucky that I married Lars six years ago because, as it turned out, I was chock full of babies!"

This, too, is not an illustration of the appeal to ignorance fallacy. After all, the identity of the biological father is not in doubt. But because Helga is ignorant of how babies are conceived, she fails to recognize that there is, in fact, a direct causal relationship between her marriage to Lars and the fact that she has given birth to five children. What she believes to be her good luck actually has a rational explanation.

We *could,* of course, view this as a rather charming feature of Helga's personality, or invoke the popular adage that "ignorance is bliss." The doctor in the following joke, however, thinks it best that his patient knows the truth:

> A 90-year-old man went to his doctor and said, "Doctor, my wife, who is 18, is expecting a baby. I'm going to be a father!" The doctor said, "Let me tell you a story. A man went hunting, but instead of his gun, he picked up an umbrella by mistake. Then, when a bear suddenly charged at him, he pointed his umbrella at the bear, shot at it, and killed it on the spot." "Impossible," said the man, "somebody else must have shot that bear." The doctor replied, "Exactly my point."

One could argue that jokes about old men fathering children are an indirect attempt to address the anxieties of younger men about the issue. In any case, although reliable data on human paternity are essentially nonexistent, a molecular geneticist at the Oregon Health Sciences University in Portland, Oregon, reports that US laboratories screening for inherited diseases typically expect to find that 10 percent of children tested are not sired by their social fathers (Morell 1998) and a spokesman for a company that sponsors projects that attempt to link different families to common ancestors states that "any project that has more than 20 or 30 people in it is likely to have an *oops* in it" (Olson 2007).

As with all fallacies, people *do* make appeals to ignorance in real-life situations and these appeals can have consequences. For example, consider this statement by Michael Griffin, NASA's administrator, in a National Public Radio interview (May 31, 2007): "I have no doubt that a trend of global warming exists. I am not sure that it is fair to say that it is a problem we must wrestle with. To assume that it is a problem is to assume that the state of the earth's climate is the optimal climate, the best climate that we could have or ever have had and that we need to take steps to make sure that it doesn't change." This is an appeal to ignorance if Griffin is making the claim that global warming is *not* a problem because there's no evidence that today's climate is optimal. As we have seen, the absence of evidence is not the same as the presence of evidence. Thus, even if there is no evidence that today's climate is optimal, this does not mean that there's evidence that today's climate is *not* optimal or that it would be a *good* thing if the climate changed. More importantly, it does not mean that we should be sanguine when faced with the prospect of climate change. After all, what you don't know *can* hurt you.

The Use of Equivocal Language

An eighth fallacy of relevance is the use of equivocal language, or using a word with multiple meanings in order to make a claim look more plausible than it really is. For example, take this apparently logical (syllogistic) argument: God is love. Love is blind. Ray Charles is blind. Therefore, Ray Charles is God. Whatever one may think of Ray Charles' singing and song-writing abilities, this argument fails to support the claim that he is God. This is because it equivocates between two different senses of the word "is." (In this sense, President Clinton was not being merely evasive or disingenuous during the investigation into his sexual relations with White House intern Monica Lewinsky when he said "that depends on what the meaning of 'is' is.")

The first sense of "is" is that of "identity," i.e., where "is" means "identical with": "God is identical with love." The second sense of "is" is that of "attribution," i.e., where "is" means "has the quality of": "Ray Charles is a blind person." This argument – that Ray Charles is God – would only work if "is" always means "identical with." This, however, is not the case because "is" has other meanings as well. This is also why equivocation is a fallacy of relevance. "Ray Charles is blind" does not mean "Ray Charles is identical with blind" (which wouldn't make any sense anyway), so this statement is irrelevant to the issue of whether or not he is God. The reason this claim may appear relevant when it really is not is because of the equivocation over the meaning "is." It is also worth noting that the word "blind" is used equivocally in this example because "blind" can mean "oblivious to" (as in "love is blind") and also "without the power of sight" (as in "Ray Charles is blind").

Many jokes depend on the equivocal use of words having multiple meanings. Puns, on the other hand, make use of the fact that various words have similar sounds. It could be argued that children make the transition from riddles to jokes when they discover the fact that words have multiple meanings (see Wolfenstein 1954, on "double meanings," pp. 63–91). Here's a joke that illustrates how equivocation works:

> **A down-and-out musician was playing the violin in the middle of a big shopping mall. He had his violin case open so that passersby could drop in donations. Then a burly security guard marched over and asked him, "May I see your permit?" "I haven't got one," the musician confessed. "In that case you'll have to accompany me." "Splendid. What shall we sing?"**

"Accompany," of course, can mean either "go with" or "play music with."

A man approaches a woman at a singles bar and asks her for her phone number. "I'm sorry," she replies, "I never give my phone number to perfect strangers." "Then we're both in luck," the man replies, "because I am far from perfect."

"Perfect" can mean either "complete" or "flawless."

A huge college freshman decided to try out for the football team. "Can you tackle?" asked the coach. "Watch this," said the freshman, who proceeded to run smack into a telephone pole and completely knocked it over. "Wow," said the coach, "I'm impressed. Can you run?" "Of course I can run," said the freshman. He was off like a shot, and in just over 9 seconds ran a 100-yard dash. "Great," the coach said. "But can you pass a football?" The freshman hesitated for a second. "Well, sir," he said, "If I can swallow it, I can probably pass it."

"Pass" can mean either "to throw through the air" or "discharge."

Bob went to his lawyer and said, "I would like to make a will, but I don't know how to go about it." "Don't worry," his lawyer replied, "leave it all to me." Bob began to get upset. "Well, I expected you to take the biggest share, but I'd like to leave a little to my wife and children, too."

"Leave it all to me" can mean "I can handle it for you" or "give it all to me."

A medical student entered a patient's room carrying a syringe. As he approached the patient's bed, he said, "Just a little prick with a needle." "I know who you are," the patient relied, "but what are you going to do?"

"Prick" can mean "a very small puncture of the skin" but it can also mean "a person regarded as contemptible or obnoxious."

An elderly woman had two small terriers, one male, the other female. When the female terrier died, the male terrier was heartbroken, and he died the next day. She took the two carcasses to the taxidermist so that they could be preserved. The taxidermist asked, "Do you want them mounted?" She replied, "No, but could you have his paw in hers?"

To the taxidermist, "mounted" meant "placed on something raised (e.g., a base or pedestal)." To the woman, "mounted" meant "to climb on top the other for copulation."

> **A judge is addressing the husband in a divorce case. "Mr. Johnson, I have reviewed this case carefully and I have decided to give your wife $2,000 a month." The husband replies, "That's very generous of you, your honor, and, believe me, I'll try to help out a little myself now and then."**

The judge is using the word "give" in the sense of "award" while the husband understands the word "give" in the sense of "personally provide."

Then there's the film actress Mae West's comment: "I was once pure as snow, but then I drifted." This quip is especially clever because it plays on the associations of "purity" with snow and with sexual innocence plus the equivocal meaning of the word "drift" ("driven by the wind" and "carried along by circumstances"). Finally, there's this rather phony syllogism – "Some dogs are friendly, my dog is friendly, therefore my dog is some dog" – which plays on the fact that in syllogisms "some" means "being of an unspecified number" but in informal conversation it can also mean "remarkable" or "striking."

The fallacy of equivocation can make a claim appear more compelling than it really is. Take, for example, the US Supreme Court case of *Plessy v. Ferguson* (1896), which was used to justify racial segregation in the United States. In that decision the Supreme Court argued that the doctrine of "separate but equal" did not violate the 14th Amendment's equal protection clause as long as there were equally good facilities for both blacks and whites. When school segregation was later overturned in the 1954 *Brown v. Board of Education* decision, the Supreme Court argued, in effect, that the earlier court had equivocated over the meaning of "equal." The Supreme Court in 1954 argued that the 14th Amendment guaranteed not just equality of facilities, or conditions, but also equality of *opportunity*. "Separate but equal" schools, it decided, were "inherently unequal" because segregation, by its very nature, deprived black students of equal opportunities. In other words, the Supreme Court argued that the authors of the *Plessy v. Ferguson* decision had committed the fallacy of equivocation by confusing two different senses of "equality": equality of opportunity (guaranteed by the 14th Amendment) and a less robust equality of condition (which "separate but equal" was designed to guarantee).

Or consider the following editorial, "Precedent is Clear," in *The Florida Union Times* (August 10, 1999) in support of banning gay Boy Scout leaders: "The Scout organization teaches traditional family values and requires its young members to take an oath to be 'morally straight.' It therefore would be hypocritical, Scout officials maintain, to allow homosexual leaders or members." Although "traditional family values" has its own ambiguities, the equivocation in this example is over the word "straight." In one sense, "straight" means "not homosexual," but in another sense, "straight" means "honest" and "direct" (e.g., calling someone "a straight shooter"). Officially, Boy Scouts swear to be "straight" in the second sense, not the first sense of the word. The Scout Oath or Promise in the *Boy Scout Handbook* includes the pledge to "keep myself physically strong, mentally awake, and morally straight," and states that "Being morally straight means to live your life with honesty, to be clean in your speech and actions, and to be a person of strong character." (See http://www.uscouts.org/advance/boyscout/bsoath.html.) The 1948 edition of the *Handbook* identifies stealing, lying, and abuse of one's body as central issues in being morally straight, and the editor of the 2004 edition of *Scouting for Boys* (originally published in 1908) by Robert Baden-Powell, the organization's founder, notes that the appendix material on self-abuse should have appeared in the body of the text but that "Baden-Powell, who had consulted with his mother about the section's inclusion, reluctantly removed it from *Scouting for Boys* under strong advice from his publisher" (p. 351). The editor believes that the publisher advised against inclusion of this material on masturbation because it was a taboo subject, though it is also possible that he was aware in 1908 that psychiatrists no longer suspected masturbation of causing mental illness. In any event, it's doubtful that the founders of the scouting movement had homosexual behavior in mind when they used the words "morally straight." However, because in our day "straight" can mean "not homosexual," the newspaper editorial avails itself of an unintended meaning of the word and commits the fallacy of equivocation.

Of course, nearly every word or term has multiple meanings and we cannot expect everyone to agree on the meaning of every word when used in verbal or written communication. Ordinarily, such disagreements are quite harmless, for often the meanings are close enough, or the different senses are obvious enough, that there is no confusion. But sometimes equivocation can make a belief or claim appear more plausible than it actually is. We are indebted to jokes for unwittingly (!) bringing this problem to our attention.

The Use of Amphiboly

A ninth fallacy of relevance is amphiboly. Amphiboly is related to equivocation but at the level of a sentence rather than a single word or term. Thus,
while equivocation depends on the different meanings of a single word or
term, amphiboly depends on different meanings of an entire sentence. Here's
a line from the Marx Brothers' film *Animal Crackers* (1930). Groucho quips:

> **One morning I shot an elephant in my pajamas. How he got into my
> pajamas I'll never know.**

The sentence "One morning I shot an elephant in my pajamas" is an example
of amphiboly. Normally, it means that a person, who was wearing pajamas at
the time, shot an elephant. But, as Groucho realizes after he says it, the same
sentence could mean that the elephant was wearing the pajamas. Changing
the sentence to read, "I was in my pajamas when I shot the elephant," would
remove the amphiboly, but it would also eliminate the joke. It's also worth
noting that this amphiboly introduces a fact that is basically irrelevant, namely,
that Groucho was in his pajamas when he shot the elephant. Not all amphiboly sentences have irrelevant clauses, but those that do reflect a characteristic
of other fallacies we have discussed, i.e., that they introduce irrelevant facts or
considerations and thus distract from what is really at issue.

Amphiboly is usually so recognizable that it is rarely used in real-life situations to make a claim seem stronger than it is. Instead, it more often leads
to humorous misunderstandings and confusions. Newspaper headlines are
one common source of amphiboly. Here are a few examples:

> **"Prostitutes Appeal to Pope" – "Farmer Bill Dies in House" – "Dr. Ruth to
> Talk About Sex With Newspaper Editors" – "Burglar Gets Nine Months in
> Violin Case" – "Juvenile Court to Try Shooting Defendant" – "Red Tape
> Holds Up New Bridge" – "Marijuana Issues Sent to a Joint Committee" –
> "Two Convicts Evade Noose: Jury Hung."**

Most likely, some of these headlines are intentional, the result of headline
editors' late night boredom. The bulletins and newsletters of religious
groups and organizations are another common source:

> **"Thursday at 5 p.m. there will be a meeting of the little mothers club. All
> ladies wishing to become little mothers please meet with the pastor in**

his study." "For those of you who have children and don't know it, we have a nursery downstairs." "The ladies of the church have cast off clothing of every kind and they may be seen in the church basement on Friday afternoon."

Newspaper advertisements are still another source:

"Drop-leaf table: The leaves when opened will seat six people comfortably and there's an automatic hinge that holds them firmly in place." "Dog for sale: eats anything, fond of children."

Signs are yet another source:

"Closing down, thanks to all our customers." "Ask about our plans for owning your home." "Automatic washing machines: Please remove all your clothes when the light goes out."

Most of these cases of amphiboly are the result of a poorly constructed sentence: "I like chocolate cake better than you." Although we normally try to avoid them, intentional amphiboly may prove useful when we feel obligated to say something we would rather not have to say, yet want to avoid saying something that is patently untrue. Here are lines from letters of recommendation: "In my opinion, you will be very fortunate to get this person to work for you." "I am pleased to say that this candidate is a former colleague of mine." From a professor on receiving a late paper from a student: "I shall waste no time in reading this."

Even as many jokes depend on an equivocal term, lots of jokes depend on amphiboly. A few examples:

A newly married man asked his wife, "Would you have married me if my father hadn't left me a fortune?" "Honey," his wife replied sweetly, "I'd have married you no matter who left you a fortune."

A doctor said to his patient, "I can't find the cause of your illness," then paused thoughtfully and added, "but frankly I think it's due to drinking." "That's OK," replied the patient, "I'll come back when you're sober."

The phone rang at the governor's mansion at 2:00 a.m. and an aide picked up the phone. A local lawyer was calling and insisted on speaking with the governor. The aide told him to call back in the morning because the governor was asleep and he didn't want to wake him. But the lawyer insisted, claiming it was a matter of the utmost importance. Reluctantly, the aide agreed to wake up the governor. "What is it?" grumbled the governor as he picked up the phone. "Judge Cassidy just died," the lawyer announced, "and I want to take his place." "It's OK with me," the governor replied, "if it's OK with the undertaker."

The judge looked down at Mickey Mouse, who was filing for divorce from Minnie Mouse. "Mr. Mouse," said the judge, "I'm afraid I can't grant your request for divorce. I've read the psychiatrist's report, and you simply have no grounds. Your wife is quite sane." "Sane?" squeaked Mickey. "I never said she was mad. What I said was that she's fucking Goofy!"

"Doctor, something's wrong! I'm shrinking!" "Take it easy, sir. You'll just have to be a little patient."

These jokes notwithstanding, amphiboly *can* be serious business. Consider the 2nd Amendment to the US Constitution: "A well regulated Militia, being necessary to the security of a free State, the right of the people to keep and bear Arms, shall not be infringed." Constitutional lawyers have long debated the meaning of this Amendment and particularly the function of the four phrases separated by commas. On one interpretation the first two phrases ("A well regulated militia, being necessary to the security of a free State") are merely prefatory and the rest of the amendment is "operative." This interpretation would justify fewer limits on gun ownership. On another interpretation, the first two phrases modify the rest of the amendment, so the right to bear arms is justified only by the need to maintain a militia. This interpretation would justify greater limits on gun ownership. Because of this amphiboly, the 2nd Amendment has been especially open to debate. This does not mean, of course, that its authors were being intentionally ambiguous or confusing.

Conclusion

The fallacies of relevance presented in this chapter spotlight a fundamental aspect of thinking critically. When considering whether someone has good reasons for what she or he believes, a fundamental question is whether these reasons are even relevant. If they are not relevant, then it doesn't matter if these reasons happen to be true or well supported: their irrelevance trumps whatever other virtues they may have. On the other hand, if these reasons are relevant, then that's only the beginning. The next question is whether there is good enough *evidence* to accept those reasons. For this very reason we turn in the next chapter to fallacies of evidence.

Good Point!

It is not wrong to laugh when we hear the jests of another. These jests may even be such that it would be difficult not to laugh at them. But when we ourselves jest, it is more fitting to abstain from laughter, in order not to seem to be surprised by the things that are said, nor to wonder at the ingenuity we show in inventing them.

(René Descartes)

Bad Limerick!!

There was a young student named Fred,
Who was questioned on Descartes and said:
   "It's perfectly clear
   That I'm not really here,
For I haven't a thought in my head."

V. R. Omerod

3 Fallacies of Evidence

We will be concerned in this chapter with fallacies of evidence, that is, beliefs or assertions which involve relevant but unsupported claims. What's evidence? Basically, it's something that tends to prove and/or provides ground for belief. The most public use of the term occurs in legal proceedings, where something is presented that bears on the point in question. It might be an object (the proverbial "smoking gun") or it might be a witness's statement ("I saw the defendant enter the apartment building that evening at ten o'clock"). But evidence also plays an important role in science, history, politics, religion, technology, marketing, personal disputes, etc., etc.

Sometimes we use the word evidence in the stronger sense of proof: To reprise an example we used in chapter 2 the fact that a woman is pregnant is proof that she has had sexual intercourse. Other times we use the word evidence in the weaker sense of grounds for belief: for example, a woman's husband believes that he's the one who impregnated her, but the man she has been having an affair with may believe that he's the one who impregnated her. Circumstantial evidence might be the physical appearance of the baby, or it might be her testimony that she had sexual relations with only one of the men at the time the conception would have occurred. However, because circumstantial evidence is inconclusive, a DNA test may be necessary to settle the question of the identity of the biological father. Here's a joke that illustrates the distinction:

> Mickey comes home to find Minnie and his best friend, Goofy, in bed together. Just as Mickey is about to open his mouth, Goofy jumps out of bed and says, "Before you say anything, old pal, what are you going to believe, me or your eyes?"

Based on what he sees, Mickey has all the proof he needs. Goofy, however, will try to persuade Mickey that his old friend's words will provide grounds for believing that his eyes are deceiving him.

Both senses of what evidence entails – whether "proof" or "grounds for belief" – are within the purview of critical thinking. We presented nine fallacies of relevance in chapter 2. We will present the same number of fallacies of evidence in this chapter. The fact that there are nine in each is merely coincidental.

The False Cause Fallacy

> A guy says to his doctor, "Every time I go on vacation, my wife gets pregnant. Went to France and she got pregnant. Went to Ireland and she got pregnant a second time. Went to Spain and she got pregnant a third time." The doctor said, "Have you thought of using some protection to avoid so many pregnancies?" The guy replied, "No, but I've been thinking that maybe next time I should take her with me."

In this joke, the doctor mistakes the cause of the wife's pregnancy. He thinks that she gets pregnant as a result of vacationing with her husband in Europe. In fact, she gets pregnant because she is *not* vacationing with him. Or, more accurately, she gets pregnant because, in her husband's absence, she has sexual relations with another man and this is how she gets pregnant.

The doctor commits the false cause fallacy: the fallacy of identifying something as the cause of a particular event when it really isn't. Formally, this is called the *post hoc* fallacy, which is a shortened form of the Latin phrase *post hoc, ergo propter hoc* which means "after this, therefore because of this." Simply because something happens after something else does not mean that it was the result of this something else. This is an easy fallacy to commit since we seem almost programmed to look for the causes or explanations of particular events. Of course, there's real survival value in being able to identify causes. It's important to know, for example, that it was the rotten meat that made everyone sick. Knowing causes also helps us understand the meaning of something, like why one nation declared war on another nation. If we get the cause wrong, we misunderstand what has happened. So it is important – and a characteristic of critical thinking – to be cautious whenever we identify X as the cause of Y.

Here's a joke in which different causes are ascribed to the very same behavior:

> Two Irishmen were digging a ditch directly across the street from a brothel. They saw a rabbi walk up to the door, glance around, and duck inside. "Ah, will you look at that" one digger said, "What's the world coming to when men of the cloth are visitin' such places?" A short time later, a Protestant minister walked up to the door and quickly slipped inside. "Do you believe that?" the digger exclaimed, "Why, 'tis no wonder the young people today are so confused, what with the example clergymen are setting for them." An hour went by. Then, the men noticed a Catholic priest enter the house. "Oh, what a pity," the digger said, leaning on his shovel, "One of the lasses must be ill."

Given the rather furtive behavior of rabbi and the minister, we assume that they are there for sex. This, of course, is also what the ditch digger assumes. But when the priest enters the house, he ascribes a different meaning to the behavior in question. He is rather transparently inconsistent in his reasoning. It *may* be that one of the lasses is ill, but the digger hasn't provided any evidence in support of this belief. In the absence of any evidence, we have reason to assume that the priest's motivation for being there is the same as that of the rabbi and the minister. On the other hand, the false cause fallacy should caution us against identifying causes where we lack evidence or our evidence is exceptionally weak. In such cases, we should withhold judgment until we can find out more facts. In this case, the facts are, literally, across the street. If the ditch diggers want proof, they will need to drop their shovels and enter the brothel to find out. Of course, they may have some difficulty in convincing passersby that their own motivation for entering the house is to satisfy their curiosity. However, it is not uncommon for persons engaged in research to be confronted with the expectation that they explain their interest in the subject that they have chosen to research.

As the Irish ditch-digger joke suggests, we typically commit the false cause fallacy all by ourselves. There are times, however, when a group of people commit it together:

> Four persons are riding in a train coach. A woman and her beautiful 19-year-old daughter are on one side, and facing them are an army general and his escort, an army private. The train enters a tunnel and the cabin gets dark. A kiss is heard, followed by a slap. The mother thinks, "That young

man stole a kiss from my daughter, and she slapped him." The daughter thinks, "That young man tried to kiss me and kissed my mother by mistake and she slapped him." The general thinks, "That young man stole a kiss and I got slapped by mistake." The private thinks, "I kiss the back of my hand and get away with slapping the general!"

The private knows the true cause of what happened because he was the one who caused it. He is known as the "efficient" cause. Because the others were not the efficient cause and could not see what had happened, they made inferences as to what caused the kissing sound followed by the slap. All three inferences were relevant, but all three were wrong. They based their inferences, in part, on what they knew did or didn't happen, but each also filled in their knowledge gaps with guesses, i.e., as to *who* caused *what*. We will discuss fallacies of assumption in the following chapter, but it's worth pointing out here that the private took advantage of their commonly shared assumption that if anyone would try to kiss someone, he would be the one to try it, and that he would try it on the daughter. This was a plausible assumption, but its plausibility was not enough. In fact, what actually caused the sounds they all heard was actually less plausible, and its very implausibility enabled the private to get away with it. This joke also illustrates the fact that two or more persons can collude, as it were, in the false cause fallacy, and that each may contribute differently to the erroneous conclusion drawn.

Sometimes this fallacy takes the form of a confusion of efficient and material causes, as when the National Rifle Association says, "Guns don't kill people, people do." For this event to take place, both an efficient cause (people) and a material cause (guns) are needed to produce a final cause (killing people). Thus, this statement sets up a false dichotomy, and this, in turn, leads to unwarranted claims that guns are no greater threat to human lives than, say, a plastic knife or a beach ball.

If unwarranted assumptions can lead to unsupported claims, accurate claims – claims that do not commit the false cause fallacy – may produce different or even conflicting conclusions. Here's a joke that illustrates this point:

A professor of medicine, a man well-known for his view that alcohol is damaging to one's health, was lecturing his medical students on the damage that alcohol can do. To demonstrate its effects on the nervous system, he took a worm and dropped it into a glass of gin and tonic. The worm wriggled around for a few minutes before finally giving a few convulsive twitches and then died. "What can we deduce from that?" the professor asked with a triumphant air, assuming the conclusion was obvious. A voice called out from the back of the lecture hall, "If you've got worms, drink alcohol!"

The professor and the student agree that the worm's demise was caused by alcohol. Their differences are in the conclusions they draw from this demonstration of causality. Many political debates occur because effects have been attributed to false causes. Many others occur because there is disagreement over the meaning or significance of true causes.

Here's a joke that illustrates a somewhat different problem: a cause is ascribed to an "event" that didn't actually happen:

> Two six-year-old boys were attending religious school and giving the teachers problems. The teachers had tried everything to make them behave – time-outs, notes home, missed recesses – but could do nothing with them. Finally the boys were sent to see the priest. The first boy went in and sat on a chair across the desk from the priest. The priest asked, "Son, do you know where God is?" The boy just sat there. The priest stood up and asked, "Son, do you know where God is?" The boy trembled but didn't say anything. The priest leaned across the desk and again asked, "Do you know where God is?" The boy bolted out of the chair, rushed past his friend in the waiting room, and ran outside the school. His friend chased after him and finally caught up with him. "Billy, tell me, what happened in there?" Billy replied, "It's awful. God is missing, and they think we're to blame!"

As the false cause fallacy assumes the event but makes an error as to the cause, this joke is not directly illustrative of the fallacy. On the other hand, it alerts us to the fact that the degree to which we consider ourselves culpable is a direct reflection of the happening that we believe ourselves to have caused. It is one thing to engage in disruptive behavior in class, and quite another to be held responsible for the disappearance of the one who is considered by many to be the cause of everything that exists.

As noted above, it's important to be cautious whenever we identify Y as the cause of X. It's equally important that we make the effort to identify the real cause or causes of X. Of course, we can avoid committing the false cause fallacy by refusing to think about causality at all. The doctor in the joke about the pregnant wife might say to himself, "Medically speaking, the important thing is that she got pregnant. How she got pregnant is of no concern of mine." For some events in life, this is a reasonable approach to take: "The bus was late this morning. Let the other passengers speculate about the reasons why it was late. All that matters to me is that I won't get to work on time."

But the search for causes is an integral part of being a critical thinker. The critical thinker operates on the belief that there's an explanation for everything, it's just that we don't always know what it is. In other words, things don't just happen, they are caused to happen, and although we don't know the causes of everything, we *do* know that everything has a cause (McInerny 2005, p. 32). Also, knowledge of causes can be satisfying from a theoretical point of view because knowing the causes of things is one of the ways we understand them. What they do or cause to happen is another. But the knowledge of causes also has practical implications, for in many ways knowing causes enables us to control them, and to control causes is to control effects. So, if we know that a certain bacterium is the cause of a particular disease, we may be able to eliminate the disease by negating the causal activity of the bacterium. This being so, we shouldn't stop short in our search for causes.

Here's a concrete example: Sam notices a foul odor in the kitchen. Investigating, he discovers that a bucket placed in the cabinet under the sink is filled to the brim with reeking water. Once he empties the bucket, the stench is gone. But it gradually returns as the bucket fills up again. Now, Sam could continue to empty the bucket on a regular basis to meet the problem of the bad smell but we would be inclined to give him rather low marks for intelligence if he were to remain satisfied with this solution. The only way to solve the problem once and for all is to get at the root of it and fix the leaky pipes that are causing the bucket to fill up. Why might Sam fail to get at the root cause? Well, he could be lazy, although it probably requires more effort to empty the bucket on a regular basis than to fix the leaky pipes. Or he could be impatient and decide to settle for a "quick-fix" or stop-gap measure (McInerny 2005, pp. 34–5).

This very question about Sam's failure to deal with the root cause of the problem raises an issue that commonly arises in efforts to get at the root cause of a happening or event: is the cause internal or external? "The devil made me do it" is an attempt to shift the locus of causality from the first to the second. Here's a joke that does the reverse:

A guy met a woman at work and asked her out on a date. When he arrived at the address she had given him, he discovered that she lived on the tenth-floor of a high-rise apartment building. While she was in her bedroom

making last minute preparations, he amused himself by tossing a ball to her pet terrier. After a few tosses toward the wall, he tossed the ball toward the patio door, which happened to be open. The dog chased after it, only to go skidding across the terrace and over the railing, falling ten stories below. When his date came out to the living room, he asked, "Has your dog been kind of depressed lately?"

By intimating that the dog had suicidal tendencies, the guy hopes to get himself out of a rather dicey situation. What happened is clear: the dog fell to his death. What could be unclear is the reason why he did so. Was he the sole agent of his plunge (an internal cause) or were there other (external) agencies involved: the guy, the ball, the game with the ball, etc. His date will probably put two-and-two together as she runs down to find her pet terrier lying on the pavement below with the ball in his mouth. And when she does, it's likely that whatever the guy planned for the evening will not take place. What *will* take place will depend on her response (internal) to what has already taken place.

Finally, we'd like to emphasize that the "false-cause fallacy" is especially a problem when the persons who make it are in positions of influence or responsibility where their errors affect the lives of others. This applies, of course, to the National Rifle Association, but it also applies to parents who think that negative feedback is better than positive feedback. If the Irish ditch diggers get it wrong, no real harm is done. But if persons who have influence or responsibility get it wrong, other people may suffer. And that's a good reason for us to be able to identify the "false cause" fallacy and do what we can to challenge those, including ourselves, who commit it.

Hasty Generalizations

A second fallacy of evidence is the hasty generalization. A generalization is the act of formulating general principles or inferences from particulars. The statement, "If this match, which I have just broken, had been scratched, it would have lit," involves a generalization: When matches are struck, they light. This happens to be a true generalization because scratched matches do in fact light. So, even though this particular match didn't light, the person who made this statement had good reason to make it: there was no reason to think that this match would have been any different from all other matches. The "hasty generalization" fallacy occurs when one makes a generalization on the basis of a limited number of instances or cases or of a sample that is not representative of the whole. The word "hasty" is somewhat misleading because the issue is not the speed with which one makes the generalization but the weakness of the evidence that supposedly supports it. In effect, one makes a big claim on the basis of too little evidence.

If someone were to say that the big-party presidential candidate who has the longest name will be elected president, and then predict the outcome of the next election on this basis, she would have been on solid ground from 1920 to 1960, four decades in which the candidate with the longest name did win the election. But between 1960 and 2004, she would have been wrong about half the time. It would therefore be a mistake to make the generalization that the big-party presidential candidates with the longest name will win the election.

The hasty generalization is very common. In many disputes, one person will cite an example as proof that it applies to all cases. For example, the columnist David Brooks (2007) relates his conversation with a truck driver in a diner in Caroline County, Virginia. Brooks points out that the truck driver has one of those hard jobs, like mining and steel-working, that, unlike jobs performed in front of a computer keyboard, supplies "a code of dignity." As the truck driver spoke, Brooks was reminded of a book by the sociologist Michele Lamont (2002) who interviewed working-class men, and described what she calls "the moral centrality of work." Her subjects placed tremendous emphasis on working hard, struggling against adversity and mastering their craft. When they looked at professionals and managers, they didn't necessarily see their social superiors. Instead, they saw manipulators. In contrast, they defined themselves as straight-talking, shoot-from-the-hip guys, and dismissed people who work in offices, who work by persuasion, as insincere, as playing games. Brooks concludes that class conflicts are less about economics and more about morals. The truck driver represented a class whose protests "are directed not against the rich, but against the word manipulators – the lawyers, consultants and the news media."

Brooks' claim that class conflicts are less about economics and more about morals may well be correct, but what is relevant here is that Lamont's subjects commit the fallacy of hasty generalization. No doubt, some people who work in offices are manipulators, even as some truck drivers are, no doubt, manipulators. But not all people who work in offices are manipulators. In fact, it's safe to say that many are just as committed to "the moral centrality of work" as truck drivers, and just as concerned as truck drivers to struggle against adversity and to master their craft.

It's worth noting that lawyers head the list of the "word manipulators." As we have already seen, jokes about lawyers are very common, and there is no other profession that is pilloried in the world of jokes as much as the legal profession. Among the negative qualities attributed to them, the most common is that they are heartless, utterly without feeling. For example:

> An associate who had worked for a Wall Street law firm for five years was working late in his office one night when suddenly there was a flash of light and a tower of smoke bursting from the floor. Satan stepped out of the smoke and addressed the lawyer: "I understand that you would give absolutely anything to make partner," Satan said, "so I've come here to make you an offer. I'll see to it that you are made partner, but in return I will claim the souls of your wife, your parents, your children, and your future grandchildren." The lawyer looked strangely puzzled and thought hard for several minutes. Finally, he turned to Satan and asked, "So what's the catch?"

Here's another:

> A priest, a doctor and a lawyer were playing golf together one morning, but were stuck behind a particularly slow group. All three were complaining about how long the group was taking on each hole. Finally, they spotted the greenskeeper, so they decided to have a word with him. "That's a group of blind firefighters," he explained. "They lost their sight while saving our clubhouse last year, so we let them play here any time free of charge." The priest said, "That's so sad. I'll say a special prayer for them tonight." The doctor said, "That's a good idea, and I'm going to consult all my textbooks to see if there isn't anything that can be done for them." The lawyer said, "Why can't these guys play at night?"

And another:

> One day it came to the attention of the chairman of the United Way that the fund had never received a donation from the most successful lawyer in town. He called on the lawyer. "Our research shows that you made a profit of over $600,000 last year, and yet you have not given a dime to the community charities." The lawyer replied, "Did your research also show that my mother is dying after a long illness, and has medical bills that are several times her annual income? Did your research uncover anything about my brother, the disabled veteran, who is blind and in a wheelchair? Did it mention my sister, whose husband died in a traffic accident, leaving her

penniless with three children?" Sheepishly, his caller admitted that he had no knowledge of any of this. "Well, since I don't give any money to them, why should I give any to you?"

The joke that summarizes the point of all these heartless lawyer jokes is the one about the heart of a lawyer being extremely expensive for persons needing a heart transplant because it has never been used. At the risk of appearing naïve, we think that this rap against lawyers in the world of jokes is an excellent illustration of the fallacy of hasty generalization. Obviously, there are many decent, caring, and selfless lawyers who have done an enormous amount of good. In addition, the fact that we have presented so many lawyer jokes throughout this book testifies to the fact that there is an affinity between this profession and established standards of rationality; and because these standards tend to reject emotional appeals (consider, for example, the appeal to pity fallacy) the heartless attribution is not altogether surprising.

Finally, it's important to note that even for true generalizations exceptions may occur. When you buy some new light bulbs, you assume that all of them will light up, but occasionally one of them is defective and it doesn't light up. The following lawyer joke makes this point:

When lawyers die, why are they buried in a hole 24 feet in the ground? It's because deep down, they are all really nice people.

Unfortunately, this joke also commits the fallacy of hasty generalization. Just because a lot of lawyers are really nice people deep down, this doesn't mean that all of them are. One needs to judge them on a case by case basis.

Lawyers, of course, are not the only stock characters in the world of jokes: blonde women, especially if they are young, are another. An underlying assumption is that blonde-haired women are not very bright in a rather harmless sort of way. For example, a blonde gets excited when one soda can after another comes out of a vending machine when she puts money into it, and she refuses to allow another customer to get a soda because she's on a winning streak. But here's a joke in which a lawyer's effort to exploit her lack of intelligence backfires:

A lawyer and a blonde were seated next to each other on a long flight from Los Angeles to New York City. He asked her if she would like to play a fun game. She refused because she wanted to sleep, but he persisted and explained that the game was really easy and a lot of fun: "I ask you questions, and if you don't know the answer, you pay me, and vice versa." She politely declined and tried to get some sleep. But he kept at her: "Okay, if you don't know the answer, you pay me $5, and if I don't know the answer, I pay you $50." He figured that since she was a blonde he would easily win the match. This proposal caught her attention and figuring that there would be no end to his badgering, she agreed to the game. He asked the first question, "What's the distance from the earth to the moon?" She didn't say a word, but reached into her purse and handed a $5 bill to the lawyer. Now it was her turn. She asked the lawyer, "What goes up a hill with three legs and comes down with four?" He looked at her with a puzzled expression. He took out his laptop computer and searched all through his references. He tapped into the air phone with his modem and searched the Internet and the Library of Congress. Frustrated, he sent e-mails to all his coworkers and friends – all to no avail. After an hour or so, he awoke the blonde and handed her $50. She took the $50 then turned away to go back to sleep. More than a little miffed, the lawyer tapped her on the shoulder and asked, "Well, so what *is* the answer?" Without a word, she reached into her purse and handed him a $5 bill, then went back to sleep.

Jokes about blondes might appear to be another example of the hasty generalization. Instead, they enable us to make a distinction between a hasty generalization – which is based on a limited number of instances or cases that are not representative of the whole – and a claim that has absolutely no evidence to support it. There *is* evidence that some lawyers are in fact heartless but there is no evidence to support the belief that there is a relationship between hair color and intelligence. Someone might say that this joke would not be as funny if the woman were a brunette or a redhead, but that's beside the point.

Failure to Take Context into Account

A third fallacy of evidence is the failure to take the context into account. In chapter 1 we noted that a belief or action can make sense in one context and not in another. Here are two jokes that reflect the fallacy of failing to take contextual factors into account when making a claim or stating a belief: We discussed the first joke in chapter 2 as an illustration of the appeal to pity fallacy. It's relevant here too:

A lawyer appealed to the judge to have mercy on his client, a young man who had murdered his father and mother: "May I remind you, your honor, that this poor fellow is an orphan."

> A doctor had just made love to one of his patients. He was feeling a bit guilty because he thought it wasn't really ethical to engage in sexual intimacies with a patient. However, a little voice in his head said, "Lots of other doctors have sex with their patients so it's not like you're the first ..." This made the doctor feel a bit better until another voice in his head said, "On the other hand, they probably weren't veterinarians."

As we noted in our earlier comments on the first joke, the lawyer conveniently overlooks or seeks to minimize the fact that the defendant is the reason he's an orphan. This is an obvious contextual issue that the lawyer obscures by asking the judge to have mercy on the defendant. With regard to the second joke, making love with a human patient is clearly a breach of professional ethics. Although the obvious point to make about the second joke is that making love to an animal is an act of perversity, it's also worth noting that the ethical question applies here as well, for it's doubtful that the doctor could possibly claim that the sexual act was consensual. In both cases, the context is an important factor in how we view the evidence: in the first case, the fact that the lawyer's client is an orphan, and, in the second case, the fact that the doctor is a veterinarian.

The first joke is worth scrutinizing a little more closely, however, because there *could* be another contextual factor that has bearing on the case, namely, that his parents were abusive and he killed them in self-defense. In this case, most people would say that this is a more important contextual reason for asking the judge to have mercy on the defendant than the fact that he is an orphan. After all, judgments about a defendant's culpability frequently take extenuating circumstances into account. In the nineteenth century, many southern states enacted laws declaring that if a husband found his wife in bed with another man and shot them both, this was justifiable homicide. In northern states legal codes treated such cases as acts of murder. The southern states took into account a contextual factor – the husband's rage – that the northern states considered irrelevant to the resulting behavior. Or, more accurately, the northern states' legal code was apparently based on the belief that a man could control his rage and find other ways than murder to redress his grievance against his wife and her lover (Stearns 1989, pp. 26–30). One of these options would be his power to have his wife committed to a mental institution (Wood 1994; Geller and Harris, 1994).

In this example, contextual factors occur on two different levels. One is the factor of jealous rage and whether the person who has this emotion should or should not be expected to be capable of controlling it. Another is the contextual factor of geographical location, and whether the act of homicide occurred in a southern or a northern state. It's important to note that the southern states and the northern states agreed that homicide is wrong, and that neither defended premeditated murder. Where they disagreed was whether homicide in this instance – finding one's wife having sexual relations with another man – was *justifiable* homicide. The southern states thought that extenuating circumstances should be taken into account. The northern states disagreed.

So just because contextual factors are an important aspect of critical reasoning, this does not mean that everything is relative. The point at issue here, though, is that the context is *relevant* to the claim or belief. In this regard, it's worth noting that jokes usually don't spell out the contextual factors that make them funny. Instead, there's an implicit assumption that the listener knows what they are or should know what they are. There may also be an assumption that making the contextual factors explicit will ruin the joke. Here's an example:

> Mama Stork, Papa Stork, and Baby Stork sat down to dinner and Mama Stork said, "What did you do today, Papa?" Papa Stork replied, "I was out making someone very happy." Mama Stork said, "I was out making someone very happy, too. What were you doing, Baby?" Baby Stork replied, "I was out scaring the crap out of college students."

To "get" the joke, you need to know two contextual things: One is the old myth that storks deliver babies. The other is the fact that coeducational college dorms have made it possible for more college students to have sex together.

Suppressing Relevant Evidence

A fourth fallacy of evidence is the suppression of evidence. It occurs when facts that are relevant to a claim or belief are intentionally withheld. Here's a joke that illustrates how this fallacy works:

> In an accident at a railroad crossing, a train smashed into a car and pushed it nearly four hundred yards down the track. Though no one was killed, the driver took the train company to court. At the trial, the signalman insisted that he had given the driver ample warning by waving his lantern back and

forth for nearly a minute. He even stood and convincingly demonstrated how he had done this. The court believed his story, and the suit was dismissed. "Congratulations," the lawyer for the train company said to the signalman when it was over, "you did a great job under cross-examination." "Thanks," he replied, "but that lawyer sure had me worried. I was afraid he was going to ask me if the lantern was lit!"

This joke illustrates the fallacy of suppressed evidence because the signalman leaves out the very fact that would have supported the car driver's case that the train company was guilty of negligence. He implies that if the other lawyer had thought to ask him if the signal was lit, he would have been forced to say that it was not, but he was not about to volunteer this information. What he said was true – that he waved the lantern back and forth – but he did not tell the whole truth.

The word "suppressed" implies, therefore, that the person who commits this fallacy has made a conscious, deliberate decision to deceive. The signalman's demonstration of how he "warned" the driver by waving the lantern back and forth was part of the deception. Often, the most effective way to succeed in the suppression of evidence is to create the appearance that one is engaging in full disclosure.

The fallacy of suppressed evidence is a particular temptation for researchers whose hypotheses are not supported by the data that they have collected and for corporations that have a lot to lose if their own research studies demonstrate that their products are defective or have negative side effects. Also, some research studies actually require the suppression of evidence relating to the very purpose of the study. For example, studies conducted by psychologists sometimes misrepresent the purpose of the study to their subjects, and justify this misrepresentation on the grounds that if the subjects knew the purpose of the study, this would unduly affect their responses and contaminate the results. Some of these misrepresentations are relatively harmless. Others do a great deal of damage and raise serious ethical questions. The following joke illustrates the problem:

A painfully shy guy went into a bar and saw a beautiful woman sitting at the bar. After an hour of gathering up his courage, he finally went over to her and asked tentatively, "Um, would you mind if I chatted with you for a while. I'm pretty lonely." She responded by yelling at the top of her lungs, "No, I won't sleep with you tonight!" Everyone stared at them and the guy was thoroughly embarrassed. He slunk back to his table. After a few minutes, she walked over to him and apologized: "I'm sorry if I embarrassed

you, but I'm a graduate student in psychology and I'm studying how people respond to embarrassing situations." To this confession, he drew up all of his courage once again and responded at the top of *his* lungs, "What do you mean, $200? Fifty is my top offer."

In this case, the graduate student's suppression of evidence – that she was conducting an experiment – was justified by her (and presumably her faculty advisors') belief that if she had informed the guy that she was conducting an experiment, he would not have responded the way he did (by slinking back to his table) and this would have invalidated her findings. On the other hand, her apology for causing him embarrassment is a bit disingenuous because the whole point of the study was to find out how subjects react to being embarrassed.

This illustration should alert us to the fact that those who suppress evidence typically claim that they have justifiable reasons for doing this. Government officials will often claim that it was necessary to suppress evidence because disclosing it would have compromised national security, sensitive negotiations, and the like. Sometimes these claims are legitimate; other times they are merely self-serving.

An especially interesting example of the suppression of evidence are cases where the one doing the suppressing claims to be acting in the best interests of the other person because the other person is "better off" not knowing the facts that are being suppressed. For centuries, this has been a common argument of members of the health profession. Why tell patients that they have a fatal illness because this will just get them upset? But this argument has been challenged on legal and moral grounds in recent decades. In the case of *Canterbury v. Spence*, the District of Columbia Circuit Court stated that "the patient's right of self decision shapes the boundaries of the duty to reveal," and this being the case, the safeguarding of patients' interest in achieving their own determination on treatment requires that the law itself will set the standard for adequate disclosure (Dworkin 1988, p. 101).

This line of reasoning led to the principle of informed consent. The patient's autonomy is the fundamental moral issue in the matter of informed consent. Decisions about what form of treatment to undergo, the probabilities of cure and of side-effects, judgments about how the body will look to others after various forms of surgery, and whether to spend one's last days in a hospital or at home are not technical matters of medical judgment. To believe that they are is a denial of the autonomy of the patient, and is especially damaging to the patient's autonomy for two fundamental reasons: first, unlike one's house or car, one's body is irreplaceable and inescapable; second, one's body is, in fact, integral to who one is. Possible exceptions to the principle of informed consent include emergency, incompetence of the patient, and therapeutic privilege. In principle, the first two are relatively unproblematic, but in certain instances there may be difficulties in determining when they apply. The third is quite problematic because it most directly infringes on the patient's autonomy and poses the greatest problems for justifying an exception. The basic point, however, is a rather simple one: namely, that, a person's autonomy is the fundamental moral issue in the matter of informed consent, and respect for one's autonomy takes precedence over other reasons for suppressing evidence, however altruistic these reasons may be (Dworkin 1988, pp. 113–16).

Finally, as the principle of informed consent recognizes, there may be occasions, however rare these may be, when suppression of evidence is justified. The following joke is a case in point:

> A cowboy goes into a bar after riding his horse into a new town. Unfortunately, the locals have a habit of picking on strangers. When he finishes his drink, he finds that his horse has been stolen. He goes back into the bar, flips his gun in the air, and catches it above his head without even looking, and fires a shot into the ceiling. "Which one of you sidewinders stole my hoss?" he yells with surprising forcefulness. No one answers. "All right, I'm gonna have another beer, and if my hoss ain't back outside by the time I finish, I'm gonna do what I done in Texas! And I don't want to have to do what I done in Texas!" He has another beer, walks outside, and his horse is back! He saddles up and starts to ride out of town. The bartender wanders out of the bar and asks, "Say, partner, before you go … What did you do in Texas?" The cowboy turns back and sighs, "I had to walk home."

Most people would agree that the cowboy had every right not to disclose what actually happened in Texas. Why? Unlike the signalman who withheld vital evidence relating to the train accident, the cowboy was the victim in this case. From a moral or ethical point of view, he was in the right and the townspeople were in the wrong. Therefore, his decision to leave them in the dark was thoroughly justified.

The Gambler's Fallacy

A fifth fallacy of evidence is the gambler's fallacy, which is the belief that an event is more likely to take place because it has not happened recently: for example, flipping a coin four times, having it come up heads each time, and then concluding that it is more likely to come up tails the next time. Parents whose first two children are boys are likely to assume that there is a greater likelihood that the third will be a girl. If the third child is a boy, they are likely to assume that the chances are even greater that their fourth child will be a girl. If the fourth child is also a boy, they may reverse their previous expectations and believe that they are fated to have all boys and no girls, a belief that may or may not be confirmed by their fifth child.

Here's a joke that sort of illustrates the gambler's fallacy:

> Pete and Eddie met in a bar after work for a drink, and began watching the six o'clock news. A man was shown threatening to jump from the Brooklyn Bridge. Pete bet Eddie $50 that the guy wouldn't jump and Eddie replied, "I'll take that bet!" The man jumped, so Pete gave Eddie the $50. Eddie said, "Hey, I can't take this. You're my friend." Pete said, "No way, a bet's a bet." But Eddie said, "Look, I have to admit, I saw the story on the five o'clock news, so it wouldn't be right for me to take your money." Pete replied, "To be honest, so did I, but I didn't think the guy was stupid enough to jump again."

What makes this joke rather implausible is that it presents a guy, Pete, who doesn't appear to know that news programs repeat footage used in an earlier broadcast and believes that a guy couldn't jump off a bridge and not only survive but also be in good enough condition to do it again an hour later. We said that the joke "sort of" illustrates the gambler's fallacy because the fallacy would require that there is an established *pattern* of repeated events. The joke would be a better example of the gambler's fallacy if Pete and Eddie were sitting in the bar watching the ten o'clock news and Pete has already watched the five o'clock and the six o'clock news and watched the man jump each time. Even better, the two guys are watching the twelve o'clock news and Pete has already watched the man jump three times. He's thinking, "No man in his right mind will repeat that performance a *fourth* time!"

But even with these revisions of the joke, it still doesn't exactly illustrate the gambler's fallacy because, in point of fact, the man doesn't jump two, three, or even four times. Instead, he only jumps once. The only way that this joke could be a true illustration of the gambler's fallacy would be if the guy jumps, survives the jump, goes back to try it again, etc. So here's a joke that does a better job of illustrating the gambler's fallacy:

> A guy goes into a bar and sees a friend at a table drinking alone. Approaching the friend he comments, "You look terrible, what's the problem?" "My mother died in June," he says, "and left me $10,000." "Gee, that's tough," he

replies. "Then in July," the friend continues, "my father died, leaving me $50,000." "Wow, two parents gone in two months, no wonder you're depressed." "And last month my aunt died and left me $15,000." "Three close family members lost in three months? That's sad." "Then this month," continues the friend, "nothing!"

This joke illustrates the gambler's fallacy of assuming that the pattern of events is connected. What makes the joke interesting is that one guy (the sympathetic friend) thinks the pattern is unfortunate while the other guy (the supposedly bereaved) thinks it's great. The guy who thinks it's been great is, of course, the one who is sorry it didn't continue.

How do we know that the gambler's fallacy is really a fallacy? Because it is based on the so-called "law of averages," that in a series of events the possible outcomes will tend to "average" out. For example, if there has been a preponderance of unfavorable outcomes in one part of a sequence, the "law of averages" would predict that there will be a preponderance of favorable outcomes in another part of the sequence. But this inference overlooks the fact that each outcome in the series is independent of its predecessors. In the coin toss, the coin has no memory of its past performances, and does not keep count in order to preserve its "average." Mathematically, whatever preponderance has been observed is of less and less significance as the number of cases increases: as a result, there is nothing to be "averaged out" (Kaplan 1964, pp. 224–5).

But might one counter: "Granted that each outcome in the series is independent of its predecessors, but isn't it the case that some outcomes are more likely than others?" Theories of probability support this counter-argument. There are various types of such theories. Mathematical probability is one of them and its clearest application is to gambling games. The mathematical probability that a player in a seven-card-stud game may make a flush (five cards of the same suit) or a straight (five cards in numerical sequence, regardless of suit) after being dealt four cards, all of which are spades, can be computed, and the odds in this case are somewhat less than 3 to 1 in favor of either of these two outcomes (Kaplan 1964, pp. 225–7).

But unless you are relying on your gambling income to pay for your college expenses, the ability to compute mathematical probabilities relating to card playing is unlikely to be of much interest to you. More important would be probabilities relating to real-life events, and for these, the assumption that they are the same as mathematical probabilities would be a serious mistake. In fact, this would be to commit the fallacy of failing to take the context into account. Consider, for example, the probability that two first cousins have the same last name. You might begin with the assumption that there are four ways in which the cousins can be related: the two mothers are sisters, or the mother of one and the father of the other are sister and brother, or the other way around, or else the two fathers are brothers. You may conclude that only in the last case will the cousins have the same last name, so the probability of their having the same last name would be one in four. The problem with this reasoning is that a large number of assumptions are being made in this calculation, and some of these may be false: For example, the assumption that one always takes the surname of one's father, which may or may not be the case; that neither cousin is a married woman, or, if she is, that she does not take her husband's surname; that two people would not have the same name unless they were related; that the sex ratio in the population is equal; that the probability of someone marrying is equally affected by the prior marriage of a brother as of a sister; and many others (Kaplan 1964, pp. 227–8).

Huntington's disease is an especially tragic situation for which probabilities are relevant. This is an inherited progressive degenerative disease of cognition, emotion, and movement. The disease affects men and women equally and is transmitted by a single dominant gene on the short arm of chromosome 1. Because the gene for Huntington's disease is dominant, having only one copy of the abnormal gene, inherited from one parent, is sufficient to cause the disease. Most people who have the disease have only one copy of the abnormal gene, and people who have only one copy of the abnormal gene may pass either the abnormal gene or the normal gene to a child. Which gene is passed on is the crucial question – the odds are 50-50. A few people have two abnormal genes; their children always inherit the disease. Because Huntington's disease begins subtly and is therefore difficult to detect in its early stages, the exact age at which it begins is difficult to determine but symptoms usually become obvious between the ages of 35 and 40 and death, often precipitated by pneumonia or by a fall, usually occurs 13 to 15 years after symptoms begin. Persons who have a parent with Huntington's disease can find out whether they have inherited the gene for the disease by taking a genetic test, but the question whether persons with a family history of the disease but no symptoms should be tested is controversial. Some persons want to know, others do not (Beers 2003, pp. 553–4).

This disease presents a difficult moral dilemma: for example, should persons who have a parent with Huntington's disease have children of their own? What makes this moral dilemma especially difficult is the fact that the odds of contracting the disease are exactly 50-50 and that symptoms do not become obvious until age 35–40, when many significant life decisions have already been made. Thus, although genetics determines the outcome, the possibility that one might be afflicted at some point in the future makes critical thinking more, not less, important and relevant.

The gambler's fallacy also raises the issue of skill vs. luck. Consider bond traders who work for investment banks: Some of them simply execute orders to buy and sell bonds on behalf of their clients, but others trade on behalf of the bank's own account. Some of the latter make vast sums of money for the banks that employ them, and banks give these "star traders" massive salaries and bonuses. But is their success due to skill or to luck?

There are a couple of ways to answer this question. If it's skill, the successful trading should persist and continue over many trades and through various market conditions. Or, you can focus on the information that is available to the trader and on how he makes his decisions. The problem is that the bond markets are more complex than a game of cards, and this complexity makes it difficult to know whether or not a trader's decision-making processes could possibly give him any advantage. Generally speaking, the investment banking industry tends to assume that a run of success is evidence of skill, and is especially likely to assume that a large win – say, $500 million – is evidence of skill when it may instead be evidence of the trader's high tolerance for risk-taking. The industry may also implicitly operate on the gambler's fallacy, believing that an early run of successes will inevitably be followed by a failure or two, thus leading the bank managers to be excessively tolerant of a trader's first couple of failures (Whyte 2005, pp. 117–123).

But if luck plays a significant role in outcomes, are we its helpless victims? Not necessarily. As Nicholas Rescher (1995) points out, we can make good, rational sense of luck: "Can a world in which things go well or ill for us fortuitously and by mere chance be coherently understood? The answer is: Of course." After all, an important achievement of reason is to grasp things as they actually are, and in a world in which contingency and ignorance are realities and chance and the unforeseeable are facts of life, reason can come to terms with this state of affairs (p. 201). In one sense, chance is reason's primary enemy, but in another sense, reason can recognize this very fact, and respond accordingly: "Reason and prudence are our best line of defense against ill luck" (p. 201). Here's a joke that illustrates Rescher's point:

> **A farmer was out in the field one morning when, much to his surprise, a dog came ambling along and said to the farmer, "Good morning," adding, "I noticed from sniffing around that you don't use pesticides." Realizing that**

he could make a fortune with a smart dog who could talk, he said to the dog, "Hey, today is Abraham Lincoln's birthday. Why don't we go to town and bet people that you can tell them whose birthday it is." The dog was amenable to this, so they climbed into the farmer's truck together. As they rode along, the dog queried the farmer about what kind of fuel he used in his truck, how many acres he owned, etc. At the local diner the farmer bet everyone $5 that the dog could tell them whose birthday it is today. But much to his chagrin, the dog just sat there and didn't say a word. On the way back, the farmer said, "I ought to whip the tar outta you. You cost me a hundred bucks back there." "It's nothing," the dog replied, "Think of the odds we're going to get ten days from now when it's George Washington's birthday!"

As far as reasoning and prudence are concerned, the dog was far out ahead of the farmer.

On the other hand, because most jokes about gambling focus on the losers, not the winners. Jokes tend to be on the side of reason, their absurdity notwithstanding, precisely because most of them focus on the losers, not the winners, and therefore caution against gambling, especially in a context where the odds are stacked against you. Here's one example:

Heading to Las Vegas, an attractive woman met a handsome young man and went gambling with him. They stopped by the roulette wheel. "What number do you think I should play?" she asked. "Why not play your age?" he suggested. Smiling, she put $100 on 27. The ball spun around, landing on 36; she promptly passed out.

Here's another:

An out-of-towner lost all of his money at the gaming tables on his first day in Atlantic City. Since he had booked a hotel room for the weekend, he stayed around and bet mentally. In no time flat, he lost his mind as well.

And, finally, here's an amusing observation that puts this whole discussion of the gambler's fallacy into proper perspective:

The optimist says that the glass is half full. The pessimist says that the glass is half empty. The rationalist says that the glass is too large.

Whereas the optimist and pessimist's observations result in a stalemate, the rationalist's observation is one on which everyone can agree, and this is no small achievement.

Affirming the Consequent/Denying the Antecedent

A sixth fallacy of evidence is called "affirming the consequent" and a seventh fallacy of evidence is called "denying the antecedent." We will be discussing the two of them together because, in books on logic, whenever one comes up, the other does too. To show how these fallacies work, we need to say a few words about conditional or hypothetical arguments. This type of argument is based on the if/then structure: if p then q. In general, what follows the "if" is called the antecedent and what follows the "then" is the consequent. So, in this case "p" is the antecedent and "q" is the consequent. Take our earlier example ("false cause fallacy") of the National Rifle Association's claim: "Guns don't kill people; people kill people." We can illustrate these two fallacies in this way. First, start with this valid statement: (1) if there's a gun around, someone can get killed. Now, here's where the trouble begins. From (1) the following, similar looking statements do *not* follow: (2) since there's no gun around, there's no way someone can get killed; (3) since someone got killed, there must have been a gun around. Statements (2) and (3) are fallacious. In particular, (2) denies the antecedent of (1) while (3) affirms the consequent of (1).

What's wrong with saying that since there's no gun around, there's no way someone can get killed (statement 2)? The problem with saying this is that it makes an incorrect inference: someone could still get killed even if there's no gun around. What's wrong with saying that someone got killed so there must have been a gun around (statement 3)? This, too, makes an incorrect inference: just because someone got killed it doesn't mean there was a gun around. In other words, if (1) is true it doesn't necessarily follow that (2) or (3) are true. Perhaps they are true, but if they are it's for reasons unrelated to (1).

Or consider this joke:

> **Three men and a dog were sitting at a table playing poker. The stakes were high and an onlooker was amazed to see Rover win two hands in a row. "That's incredible," the onlooker said, "I've never seen such a smart dog before." "He ain't that smart," whispered one of the players, "Whenever he gets a good hand, he wags his tail."**

This joke plays on the distinction between being smart in the sense of basic intelligence (i.e. the fact that a dog can play poker at all is evidence of high intelligence, especially for a member of the canine species) and being smart in the sense of being a savvy poker player (i.e. for a dog, not wagging his tail would be the equivalent of a human being able to maintain a poker face).

Here, though, we're interested in the joke's relevance to the fallacies of affirming the consequent/denying the antecedent: according to the joke, (1) if Rover gets a good hand, he wags his tail. Here's where the trouble begins: from (1) it doesn't follow either that (2) because Rover didn't get a good hand, he won't wag his tail (this would be denying the antecedent) or (3) because Rover did wag his tail, he must have a good hand (this affirms the consequent). Most people will see the fallacy in (3). They will say, "He could have lots of reasons for wagging his tale (a female dog passed by, someone filled his bowl with food, etc.)." It's (2) that's likely to give people pause: it seems to follow from statement (1): "If Rover gets a good hand, he wags his tail." Doesn't it then follow that if he got a bad hand, he didn't wag his tail?" No. If you assume this then you are making an inference for which no evidence has been provided. For all we know, on the basis of (1), Rover may still wag his tail even when he gets a bad hand. Of course, for the joke to work, we need to assume that Rover is more likely to wag his tail when he gets a good hand, but that doesn't mean he never wags his tail when he gets a bad hand.

Here's another example about inferences: "If a train is traveling from Washington, DC to Boston, then it stops in New York." There's nothing problematic here. It simply states a fact. The problems emerge when you begin to make inferences: If you see a train stopped in New York, can you infer that it is traveling from DC to Boston? No. It *could* be traveling from Pittsburgh to Montreal. If you see a train stopped in New York on its way to Boston, can you infer that the train originated in Washington, DC? No. It could have originated in Philadelphia. If you see a train originating from Washington, DC, stopped in New York, can you infer that it is traveling on to Boston? No. It could be going no farther than New York.

Now, suppose the conditional is this: "If flight 409 is canceled, then passenger Jones cannot arrive on time." There's nothing problematic here. We can assume this is simply a statement of fact (if p, then q.) But problems develop if we then draw either of the following conclusions: "Since flight 409 was not canceled, passenger Jones arrived on time" and "Since passenger Jones didn't arrive on time, flight 409 was canceled." The first of these two scenarios denies the antecedent (the flight occurred); the second affirms the consequent (Jones didn't arrive on time). In the first case, you have no grounds for saying that Jones arrived on time. If the flight had been canceled, she *would* have been late, but if the flight was not canceled, she *could* have been late regardless (e.g., the flight was delayed, not canceled). In the second case, there are no grounds for concluding that because passenger Jones was late, flight 409 was canceled. Again, perhaps flight 409 was just delayed, not canceled.

Affirming the consequent

Let's focus on the fallacy of affirming the consequent. Someone might say, "If it rains on Friday (*p*), then we won't have the picnic (*q*)." Or, "If you work hard in this class (*p*), then you'll get a good grade (*q*)." The statement is called a conditional because it states that if the condition is met – rain or hard work – then certain consequences will follow – cancellation of the picnic, a good grade in class. The fallacy of affirming the consequent is committed when you contend that the only possible explanation for the consequent – the picnic *didn't* happen, you *did* get the good grade – is that the antecedent was, in fact, the case: it *did* rain on Friday, you *did* work hard in this class. But there could be other reasons why the picnic didn't take place or why you got a good grade in the class. For example, the weather might be ideal on Friday and yet, for reasons unforeseen, such as the fact that a family member dies in the meantime, the picnic doesn't take place but a funeral does. Or you may not work hard in class, but you learn on the final day of class that the professor decided to give everyone an "A" to prove that he is really a nice guy, or because he is going up for tenure and needs a lot of positive student evaluations of the course, or wants students to recommend the course to other students so that he will have impressive enrollments. Conditional arguments can be confusing because, in some cases, q is stated in the affirmative – you'll get a good grade – and sometimes in the negative – we won't have the picnic. It's useful to keep in mind that *not* having the picnic is no less a happening than having the picnic.

Because this fallacy is concerned with explaining something that happens, it is similar to the false cause/post hoc fallacy. The difference is that in this case the form of the argument is a conditional one: *if* this happens (cause) *then* this will happen (effect). In effect, the argument is a predictive one, and some predictions are better than others. For example, you improve the chances that the prediction will turn out to be the case if it is based on prior experience: last year it rained on the day we had planned to have the picnic and we decided not to have a picnic in the rain; or you have worked hard in other courses and when you have done so, you have gotten a good grade. But, as noted, just because the picnic didn't happen or you got a good grade doesn't necessarily mean that the reason for these things happening was that it rained or that you worked hard in class.

Here's a joke that illustrates this fallacy:

> A guy goes into a bar and sits down next to another guy who has a dog at his feet. "Does your dog bite?" he asks. "No," says the other guy. So the first guy reaches down to pet the dog, and the dog bites his hand. "Hey, I thought you said your dog doesn't bite!" "He doesn't, but who said this is my dog?"

The consequent in this case is that the dog bites the guy. He didn't expect to get bitten because he thought the dog at the other guy's feet was the other guy's dog and the other guy didn't make any effort to correct this reasonable assumption. We might imagine that he was thinking "If that guy lied to me, then I'll get bitten" and when the dog bit him he then concluded "that guy lied to me." So, not only does the guy who goes into the bar get bitten, but he also commits the fallacy of affirming the consequent. The other guy didn't really lie to him, though he certainly could have been more forthcoming. If someone were to point out to the first guy, "You just committed the fallacy of affirming the consequent," he might reply that committing this fallacy is rather trivial in comparison to a nasty dog bite. But next time he might be more cautious in concluding that just because you see a guy and a dog in close proximity, the dog belongs to this guy. Maybe another guy had to go to the restroom and asked the guy to watch his dog. Or maybe the guy offered to take his brother-in-law's dog for a walk and got thirsty. Or, maybe ...

Here's a joke we already presented in chapter 2 in our discussion of amphiboly. It works just as well here:

> A newly married man asked his wife, "Would you have married me if my father hadn't left me a fortune?" "Honey," his wife replied sweetly, "I'd have married you no matter who left you your fortune."

This joke is clever because the husband is trying to establish that his wife would have married him (the consequent) even if he weren't rich (the antecedent). Her rather evasive reply indicates that she probably *did* marry him because he was rich. But the joke also illustrates the fact that arguing from consequence back to antecedent is risky business: the wife affirms the consequent (she would have married him) but the way she puts it ("no matter who left you your fortune") makes it clear that we cannot, therefore, accept the antecedent that she would have married him even if he weren't rich. In this particular case, the husband might want to rephrase the question and ask his wife: "Would you have married me if I were poor?" He'd stand a better chance of getting a straight answer, but the rest of us would be one joke the poorer.

Denying the antecedent

Here's an interesting case of denying the antecedent: Nabutauntau, a village in a remote island of Fiji, has suffered from the persistence of poverty and the absence of modern developments enjoyed by other Fiji villagers. The village has no electricity and only a jungle-logging track links it to the outside world. It has been the butt of Fijian jokes for decades. The villagers themselves attribute their impoverished condition to an event that occurred in 1867, when their tribal forefathers cannibalized Rev. Thomas Baker, an Australian Methodist missionary. According to folklore, all that remained of him were his leather boots which proved too tough to eat. The villagers believe that their plight is due to revenge by Baker's restless spirit. As a result, they have apologized on several occasions. In 1993 they presented the Methodist Church of Fiji with Baker's boots, which their forebears found to be inedible. In 2003 they apologized to the family of the victim and made reparations of cows, specially woven mats and thirty carved sperm-whale teeth to his descendents. The probable reason for Baker being cannibalized is that the village chief saw Baker combing his hair and, never having seen a comb before, asked to borrow it. When the comb got stuck in the chief's hair, Baker removed it, not knowing that in Fijian custom touching the chief's head is an absolute taboo and punishable by death (Pareti 2003).

In this case, the consequent is the impoverished condition of the villagers of Nabutauntau, and the antecedent is the 1867 cannibalization of Rev. Baker which has resulted in revenge by Baker's restless spirit. We might imagine the villagers stating something like, "If Rev. Baker's spirit remains restless then we will remain impoverished." They then seem to conclude that, if Rev. Baker's spirit can be put to rest, they will no longer live in poverty. With all due respect for the beliefs of the villagers and their conviction that the only way their situation might change is by apologizing and making reparations to the religious organization that sent Baker to the Fiji islands and to his descendents, this is a case of the fallacy of denying the antecedent. Obviously, there are many other real causes of their impoverished condition, including the remoteness of the village and the prejudices of the other Fiji islanders. As a result we have to conclude that they will remain impoverished no matter how well they apologize to Rev. Baker's family. On the other hand, if no significant change results from the two apologies (in 1993 and 2003), the villagers may be able to consider other explanations for their plight and, if so, their apologies will not have been in vain.

The fallacy of denying the antecedent is the flip-side of the fallacy of affirming the consequent. If affirming the consequent claims that there's only one explanation for something happening, denying the antecedent says that if a certain event does not take place, then it follows that nothing can take place that would have been an effect of that cause. While it is true that there cannot be an effect without a cause, this fallacy overlooks the fact that a particular effect can have many different causes. Just because one cause does not take place it does not follow that they all do not. Here's a joke that illustrates this fallacy:

> Trudy brought Bobby, her new boyfriend, home to meet her parents. They were horrified by his greasy hair, tattoos, dirty language, and air of hostility. When Bobby announced at the dinner table that he had to go and take a crap, this afforded Trudy's parents a chance to express their concerns. Her mother said, "Dear, Bobby doesn't seem like a very nice person." But Trudy replied, "Mother, if he wasn't a nice person, why would he be doing 500 hours of community service?"

In addition to being a rather poor judge of character, Trudy has also committed the fallacy of denying the antecedent. We might imagine that her mother has this conditional in mind: if Bobby does bad things (swear, act hostile, etc.) then he's not a very nice person. Trudy's response is to point out that, in fact, he does do good things, concluding that he is, therefore, a nice person. But in saying this she is denying the antecedent of her mother's conditional in order to reach the conclusion that Bobby is a nice person. However, the fact that Bobby is engaging in 500 hours of community service does not mean that her mother's claim is invalid. In fact, Trudy has inadvertently contributed another reason why one might think Bobby is not a nice person.

In *Crimes against Logic* Jamie Whyte (2005) tells about how, when he was a boy, he would occasionally tell his parents about how awful he found some classmate to be. He would list the classmate's most appalling characteristics and wait for parental groans of agreement. But these were never forthcoming. Instead, they always offered some hypothesis as to why the other kid had turned out this way: his parents had divorced, he felt insecure, his father beat him mercilessly, etc., etc. Jamie would protest: Maybe so, but explaining why the classmate is awful doesn't show that he isn't awful. On the contrary, it assumes that he is. So why do you make these remarks as if they count *against* my point? If, for example, he had told his parents that there is a mountain range in Switzerland, they would not have corrected him by explaining how that mountain range came to be formed. So why the difference in argumentation when he made a observation about one of his classmates? He guesses that his parents assumed that he was morally condemning the boy in question, and that they didn't want their son to engage in such moral condemnation. Instead, they wanted him to recognize that the boy was not personally at fault for having these disagreeable qualities. In his view, however, he was not engaging in moral condemnation of the boy in question and that, in any case, this assumption was beside the point (pp. 147–8). So, in a way, they also committed a fallacy of relevance, although none of the fallacies we discussed in chapter 2 quite fits.

We'll conclude our discussion of these two fallacies with a joke from Sigmund Freud. It's one of several jokes he tells about marriage brokers, who, in his judgment, represent a tradition – the arranged marriage – which is demeaning to all concerned (Freud 1960, pp. 75, 127):

> **The bridegroom was paying his first visit to the bride's house in the company of the broker, and while they were waiting in the *salon* for the family to appear, the broker drew attention to a cupboard with glass doors in which the finest set of silver plates was exhib0ited. "There! Look at that! You can see from these things how rich these people are." "But," asked the suspicious young man, "mightn't it be possible that these fine things were only collected for the occasion – that they were borrowed to give an impression of wealth?" "What an idea!" the broker protested, "Who do you think would lend these people anything?"**

Obviously, the marriage broker's objection is no more valid than Trudy's objection that Bobby's 500 hours of community service proves that he is a nice person. It does not disprove the bridegroom's observation that the set of silver plates was borrowed. In fact, it tends to support it – or prove nothing at all.

The Fallacies of Composition and Division

An eighth fallacy of evidence is the fallacy of composition and a ninth is the fallacy of division. Like the two previous fallacies, they belong together because both of them involve inferences from parts to wholes and from wholes to parts. The fallacy of composition occurs when a person asserts that an entirety has a certain quality because its parts have that quality. The fallacy of division occurs when a person says that the parts have the same quality as the whole.

The fallacy of composition

Let's begin with the fallacy of composition. Supposing someone says that the Yankees are the best team in baseball because, man for man, they have the best players. If they make that statement, they commit the fallacy of composition. Baseball fans know that this is fallacious reasoning and they can cite many examples of when the best team "on paper" was not the best team based on games won and lost. In fact, the best team "on paper" could be a second-rate team because the players are unable to play well together. Here's another example: a car salesman can persuade you to buy a car on the grounds that the monthly charges are exceptionally low. After you take delivery of the car, you look at the deal you signed and discover that the total cost of the car is very high. The salesman didn't tell you *that* and you didn't think to ask. Here's an apparent example but really isn't: A hotel advertisement can say, "We have exceptionally large rooms," and you may choose this hotel on the basis of the advertisement, only to discover when you arrive that the hotel also has exceptionally small rooms, including the one to which you have been assigned. This is not an example of the fallacy of composition because the advertisement did not claim that all the rooms are exceptionally large; it merely failed to say that some are large and some are small.

Consider the following joke:

> After enlisting in the army, Marvin had second thoughts about serving. So when he was told to bring a urine specimen to the selective service medical officer, he filled a bottle with specimens from his father, his sister, his dog, and then a bit of his own. Striding confidently into the lab with his specimen bottle, he waited a full hour while the sample was analyzed. Finally, the technician returned. "It took some doing," she said, "but according to our analysis, your father has herpes, your sister is pregnant, your dog is in heat, and you're in the army."

In addition to being in the army, Marvin has committed the fallacy of composition. He represents the urine specimen as composed of his urine only, but the lab analysis reveals that the sample consists of urine samples from three others besides him. Had the lab technician not have been able to differentiate the producers of the four samples, Marvin's attempt to avoid military service might have worked, unless, of course, the military was so desperate for new recruits that it was willing to accept a man who had herpes, was pregnant, and in heat. Unfortunately for Marvin, his own urine sample was the only one of the four that did not raise questions about his suitability for military service.

Important as his fate may be to Marvin, we doubt that anyone would have thought of the fallacy of composition if it merely applied to situations in which a fellow produces a urine specimen that is the composite of four different contributors. In fact, interest in this fallacy, as well as the fallacy of division, which we discuss next, can be traced all the way back to the Greek philosophers and to their interest in the metaphysical problem of the one and the many, a problem that William James once noted is not one that many persons these days lose sleep over but which he, "after long brooding over it," has come to consider "the most central of all philosophic problems" (James 1987a, p. 542).

D. Q. McInerny (2005) notes that there are far more risks in moving from the particular to the universal than the other way around: "Knowledge of a part does not allow me to say anything definitive about the whole" and "in some instances, any attempt to make that move would yield a conclusion that is manifestly false" (p. 50). For example, "Some women are mothers" is a true statement, but it cannot be used to support the conclusion that every woman is a mother. The whole can contain a part, but a part cannot contain the whole. Then is there any legitimate way we can move from particular to universal? Yes, but only if we are careful not to claim anything beyond what the evidence allows us to claim. For example, if everyone you meet in County Clare, Ireland, has red hair and green eyes, you may conjecture that everyone in the village has red hair and green eyes. But you will not know for certain until you have met everyone in the village (pp. 50–1).

Consider this joke:

A large construction worker with a menacing glare enters a bar. He orders a beer, chugs it back, and bellows, "All you guys on the right side of the bar are jerks." A sudden silence descends. After a moment he asks, "Anyone got a problem with that?" No one says a word. He then chugs back another beer and growls, "All you guys on the left side of the bar are sissies." Once again

the bar is silent. He looks around belligerently and roars, "Anyone got a problem with that?" No one says a word. But a lone man on the right side of the bar gets up from his stool and starts to walk toward the man. "You got a problem, buddy?" "Oh no, sir, I'm just on the wrong side of the bar."

The construction worker's error was in claiming that everyone on the right side of the bar is a jerk. He failed to take account of the possibility that one of the guys in the "jerk" group belonged in the "sissy" group. It's worth noting that no one challenged his claim that everyone on the left side of the bar is a sissy. Maybe they were content to be classified as sissies. There's also the issue of what it means to be located in the middle of the bar. Does this mean that the construction worker is neither a jerk nor a sissy or does it mean that he is both? The fact that one could argue either way supports McInerny's point that one should not claim more than the evidence allows. In our view, there's no doubt that the construction worker is a jerk. The jury is still out on whether he is also a sissy. The mere fact that he is large and menacing does not preclude this possibility.

The fallacy of division

Let's now consider the fallacy of division. As we've said, it involves believing that the parts have a certain quality because the whole has that quality. For example, a well-written book does not necessarily consist entirely of well-written sentences. You would assume that the preponderance of sentences of a well-written book would be well written, but just as a whole lot of well-written sentences does not guarantee that the book is well-written, so the fact that the book is well-written does not mean that all of the sentences are well-written. If you were to declare, say, in a letter to the editor of your local newspaper, that the US Congress is a bunch of thugs, your own congressperson could write you a personal letter and claim that you are wrong because she is not a thug. Most likely, she would provide evidence in support of her claim, noting, for example, that she has worked tirelessly for education, health insurance reform, and the protection of endangered species. She might conclude her letter with a rhetorical flourish – something that politicians are known for – "If that makes me a thug, then I plead guilty."

Or say that you flunked a course in chemistry but your grades in all other courses have been excellent. Does the fact that you have flunked this course mean that your college performance has not been excellent? No. Your overall performance has been excellent, and the fact that you flunked a single course doesn't change that. To be sure, you would need to acknowledge that, having failed a course, you did not achieve perfection, but your failure to achieve perfection would have been true even if you had passed all of your courses.

Here's a joke that has bearing on the fallacy of division:

> A lawyer, defending a man accused of burglary, tried this creative defense: "Your honor, my client merely inserted his arm into the window and removed a few trifling articles. His arm is not himself, and I fail to see how you can punish the whole individual for an offense committed by his right arm." "Well put," the judge replied, "and using your logic, I sentence the defendant's arm to one year's imprisonment. He can accompany it or not, as he chooses."

Because the judge suggests that the lawyer is engaging in logic, this joke has particular relevance to the fallacies that we are discussing in these chapters. The lawyer does not commit the fallacy of division. In fact, he actually challenges it. He says, in effect, that the man accused of burglary is a decent, law-abiding citizen, and just because his arm committed an offense doesn't change this fundamental fact. The judge goes along with this reasoning and agrees that the man's arm is to blame for the burglary. The problem, of course, is that the man's arm is attached to his body, and the judge is betting on the likelihood that he will make the reasonable decision to join his arm in jail. If so, the defendant's response to the judge's sentence provides evidence that the fact that one is a convicted criminal does not necessarily mean that he is incapable of thinking rationally, and this may therefore be a better challenge to the fallacy of division than the lawyer's argument.

Missing the Forest for the Trees

In this chapter we have presented nine fallacies of evidence. We could have presented several more, but the ones discussed here make the case that there are lots of ways in which we make mistakes when we either try to give evidence in support of our claims or simply fail to give any evidence at all. Pointing out these fallacies and keeping them in mind when we try to think rationally can help us to be more careful about the claims that we make and the beliefs that we hold. But there can be a danger in this too. We might focus so much on the fallacies that we forget the larger issue, which is the fact that critical thinking requires that we provide evidence for what we believe. We should not miss the forest for the trees.

With this cautionary note in mind, we will conclude our exploration of the issue of evidence with a few jokes in which evidence is the key issue:

> An old guy goes to the doctor for a checkup. The doctor says, "You're in great shape for a 60-year-old." The guy replies, "Who says I'm 60?" Doctor: "You're not 60? How old are you?" "I'll be 80 next month." "Good God! 80! Do you mind if I ask how old your father was when he died?" "Who says my father's dead?" "He's not dead?" "Nope, he'll be 104 this year." "With such a good family medical history, your grandfather must have been pretty old when he died." "Who says my grandfather's dead?" "What, he's not dead?" "Nope, he'll be 129 this year, and he's getting married next week." "Good God! But why at his age would he want to get married?" The patient replied, "Who says he wants to?"

This conversation between the patient and the doctor is all about evidence. The doctor makes several erroneous inferences, all of which are wrong. The joke is funny because he gets so focused on age (a factual matter) that he jumps to a wrong conclusion about the grandfather's motivation for getting married (a values issue). The patient's repeated use of the phrase "Who says?" indicates that the doctor is basing his assertions (beliefs) on inadequate evidence. Of course, the joke presents an absurd situation. But, in doing so, it does the important service of encouraging us to base our beliefs on good, reliable evidence, and resisting the urge to believe something if we haven't taken the trouble to search for the relevant evidence.

Sometimes, though, the problem is not so much that the evidence is hard to come by, but that the evidence is unpleasant:

> Bill, Frank, and John were waiting to be cleared for entrance into heaven. St. Peter walked up to Bill and asked, "How many times did you cheat on your wife?" Bill thought for a moment and replied, "To tell you the truth, I'd say about forty times." "That's not good," St. Peter said, "But I appreciate your honesty. You may enter heaven, but you will have to drive that Yugo over there for the rest of eternity." St. Peter approached Frank and asked the same question. Frank answered, "Sir, I believe it was about ten times." "That's not so good," St. Peter replied, "but I appreciate your honesty. You may enter heaven, and you will be driving that red Buick." St. Peter went up to John and repeated the question. Without pause, John answered, "Never!" St. Peter looked at him and asked, "Never? Are you

sure?" "I have never been unfaithful to my wife," he replied. "Excellent," said St. Peter, "you may now enter heaven, and you will be driving that beautiful gold Rolls-Royce." Grinning ear to ear, John approached the car, but when he reached the car, he suddenly dropped his head on the roof and began to cry. St. Peter rushed over and asked, "What could possibly be the problem, John? I just rewarded you with the best car in the whole fleet." John looked at St. Peter and said, "Oh, it's not that. It's just that I saw my wife pass by on a skateboard!"

John does not need to have it spelled out to him what the skateboard means. In the context of conveyances for getting around heaven, the skateboard itself is all the evidence he needs. It's also all the evidence we need to "get" the joke. Sometimes the grounds (evidence) for belief are very hard to come by. Other times they are almost to clear. That's why we have the word "self-evident," and it's to their credit that the founders of our nation were not reluctant to use the word when they claimed that it is true that all persons are created equal and are endowed with certain unalienable rights.

Good Point!

The reasonings at which we laugh are those we know to be false, but
which we might accept as true were we to hear them in a dream.
They counterfeit true reasoning just sufficiently to deceive a mind
dropping off to sleep. There is still an element of logic in them, if
you will, but it is a logic lacking in tension, and, for that very reason,
affording us relief from intellectual effort.

Henri Bergson

Bad Limerick!

The philosopher Berkeley once said
In the dark to a maid in his bed:
   "No perception, my dear,
   Means I'm not really here,
But only a thought in your head."

P. W. R. Foot

4 Fallacies of Assumption

This chapter is about the third general type of fallacies – fallacies of assumption. An assumption is anything taken for granted, and is virtually synonymous with a supposition, or the act of supposing that something is true. Thus, to assume that something is true is to take it to be true without being positively certain that it *is* true. Sometimes, we need to assume certain things are true simply to get the reasoning process underway. If the process is successful its very success may allow us to confirm that what we assumed to be true is in fact true (McInerny 2005, p. 111). On the other hand, the reasoning process may reveal that what we assumed to be true was in fact false. In this case, the reasoning process has been successful even though it did not turn out as we expected it would. This is because it's more important to discover the truth than merely to prove that our assumptions were correct.

In this chapter, we will consider five fallacies of assumption. If fallacies of evidence involve relevant but unsupported claims, fallacies of assumption involve unwarranted assumptions. In other words, there are no reasonable grounds for believing them to be true, and this being the case, they do not deserve our trust or confidence even if we cannot positively disprove them. Like fallacies of relevance, an unwarranted assumption may sabotage the reasoning process from the very outset, and nothing very useful will therefore come from the reasoning process itself.

The False Dilemma

The first fallacy of assumption is the false dilemma. Our English word "dilemma" comes from two Greek words, which can be roughly translated as "two possibilities." There are, in fact, genuine either/or situations in life in which there are two and only two possibilities open to us. And there are also situations in which there are several possibilities open to us. If, in situations where there are only two possibilities and one of these possibilities is favorable and the other unfavorable, it would be rather easy to make the decision to affirm the favorable one and avoid the unfavorable one. In this case, most people would be unlikely to call the situation a dilemma. On the other hand, we may experience a dilemma when we are faced with two favorable possibilities and need to choose between them. We commit the fallacy of the false dilemma when, in a situation entailing several possibilities, we assume that there are only two. The dilemma is false because it represents a distortion of the actual state of affairs. This is a fallacy of assumption, therefore, because one assumes that there are only two possibilities when, in fact, there are three or possibly more.

Consider this example: During one of the many nineteenth-century riots in Paris the commander of an army detachment received orders to clear a city square by firing at the rabble. He commanded his soldiers to take up firing positions, their rifles leveled at the crowd, and as an awful silence descended he drew his sword and shouted at the top of his lungs: "My fellow Parisians, I have orders to fire at the rabble. But as I see a great number of honest, respectable citizens before me, I request that they leave so that I can safely shoot the rabble." In a few minutes, the square was empty and he had accomplished his orders without firing a single shot (Watzlawick, Bavelas, and Jackson 1974, p. 81).

The commander had been presented with a dilemma: fire at the crowd (which he doesn't want to do) or defy his orders (which he also doesn't want to do). By focusing on the word "rabble" and suggesting that for most of the persons in the square the word "rabble" doesn't fit, he identifies a third alternative that gets him off the horns of the dilemma. What appeared to be a true dilemma was instead a false dilemma.

In our comments in chapter 3 on the fallacy of composition, we cited a joke about a construction worker who declared that the persons on the right side of the bar were jerks and the persons on the left side of the bar were sissies. The guy who moved from the sissies side to the jerks side demonstrated that, at least as far as the jerks side is concerned, the construction worker has committed the fallacy of composition (i.e., of asserting that the whole has a certain quality because the parts have that quality). We can also say that the guy who moves from one side to the other accepts the terms of the dilemma, namely, that if you are on one side of the bar, you are a sissy, and if you are on the other side of the bar, you are a jerk. Of course, it's doubtful that he really believes that he is on the wrong side of the bar. After all, the belligerent guy hasn't offered a single shred of evidence in support of his assertion that the guys on the right side are jerks and the guys on the left side are sissies. So it's safe to assume that he has decided to play along with the false dilemma – either you're a jerk or a sissy – because it may be prudent to join the "sissies," the group that the belligerent guy would be less likely to expect to challenge him. Also, if some other guys followed his lead, moving from one side of the bar to the other, the situation could get so hopelessly confused that the irrational nature of the false dilemma would be apparent to everyone. Another option would be for the lone man to say, "I'm neither a jerk nor a sissy" and exit the bar. In so doing, he would directly challenge the fallacy of the false dilemma. A more subversive approach would be to move to the center of the bar where the construction worker is sitting and confess to him that he is uncertain where he belongs because "sometimes I'm a jerk and other times I'm a sissy."

Here's a more complicated version of the fallacy of the false dilemma:

> As a gesture to welcome his new son-in-law into the family, a successful businessman gave the younger man a half share of the firm. "From now on," the father-in-law said, "we're equal partners. All you have to do is go down to the factory each day and learn the ropes." "I couldn't do that," the son-in-law replied, "I hate factories. They're such noisy places." "That's no problem," the businessman said, "We'll put you in the office. You can oversee the cleri-cal staff." "No way," answered the son-in-law, "I'm not going to be stuck behind a desk all day." Not surprisingly, the businessman was getting irri-tated by this display of ingratitude. "I've just made you half-owner of this thriving company. First, I offer you a management position in the factory, but you don't want that. Then I offer you a management post in the office, and you don't want that. What am I going to do with you?" The son-in-law thought for a moment and said, "Well, you could always buy me out."

In this case, we could say that the son-in-law faces a real dilemma. His father-in-law's offer of half-ownership carries the stipulation that he will work for the company. So he is confronted with two unfavorable possibili-ties: Work for the company and reap the benefits of half-ownership of the company, or refuse to work for the company and risk losing half-ownership of the company. He's caught on the horns of a dilemma. Of course, the father-in-law does not think of this as a dilemma. After all, he minimizes the condition on which the half-ownership is based, suggesting that all his son-in-law has to do is go down to the factory every day and learn the ropes. What he can't appreciate (and who can blame him?) is that, for the son-in-law, the very prospect of having to work in exchange for half ownership of the company presents a genuine dilemma. The son-in-law's proposal – "You can always buy me out" – is an attempt to get himself out of the dilemma. His ingenuity in this regard indicates that he does not commit the fallacy of the false dilemma. This doesn't mean that he's a person of integrity, but that's not the issue. We're concerned here with the *assumption* that there are two and only two options available, and, like the French commander, the son-in-law challenges this assumption and comes up with a third possibility.

What makes the false dilemma worth our attention? The most obvious reason is that so many people in leadership positions use it. We've already mentioned the National Rifle Association's slogan, "Guns don't kill people. People kill people." What is a rational person to do with this slogan: Agree or disagree? In either case, one is presented with a false dilemma. Or consider the public debate in New Zealand on legalizing homosexuality (Whyte 2005). One of the most popular arguments against legalization was that homosexuality is an unnatural act and should therefore be illegal. Those who supported legalization argued that, on the contrary, homosexuality is a natural act and therefore should be legalized. So the debate focused on whether homosexuality is a natural or unnatural act. If you consider it unnatural, you come down on the side that it should be illegal. If you consider it natural, you come down on the side that it should be legal. But why allow the unnatural/natural distinction any place whatever in considering the merits of legalizing or not legalizing homosexuality? (pp. 148–50). Many behaviors are natural or unnatural depending on who is doing the behaving. For someone who has never thrown a discus or swung a golf club, both of these behaviors are unnatural. But for someone who has been doing these things for years, nothing could seem more natural. The same applies to sexual behaviors in general, and there is simply no need to treat homosexual behaviors as special or unique in this connection. In doing so, however, a false dilemma is created.

One last joke on the fallacy of the false dilemma:

A dutiful son spoke to his ailing 95-year-old mother about her funeral arrangements. He said to her, "I know this is an uncomfortable subject, Mom, but we need to make plans for your funeral. For instance, when you die, do you want to be buried or cremated?" The old woman responded brightly, "I don't know. Why don't you surprise me?"

Knowing that he is broaching an uncomfortable topic, the son tries to be sensitive to his mother's feelings. He suggests that there are two options, and asks which one she prefers. She avoids being placed in this dilemma by being evasive. A more direct response when faced with the dilemma of two unfavorable alternatives would be to say, "Oh, I forgot to tell you. I've made arrangements for my body to be donated to the medical school for scientific research." D. Q. McInerny (2005) points out that the fallacy of the false dilemma

> seeks to create a false sense of urgency in an audience, to force them to choose between the alternatives carefully selected by the perpetrator of the fallacy. This sense of urgency is especially important to achieve if neither of the alternatives being offered is particularly attractive. Let us say I present you with the alternatives of A or B. I want you to choose A. Here is how I would argue: "A, admittedly, is not all that pleasant a choice, but the only alternative you have is B, and that is awful. Certainly you would not want that!" (p. 125)

In this respect, you have to admire a 95-year-old woman who doesn't feel the urgency that her son feels. Given the alternatives he presents her with, she tells him, in effect, that she can wait. And sometimes this is the difference between thinking rationally or irrationally.

Begging the Question

A second fallacy of assumption is begging the question. Formally, it is known as *petitio principii*. It means that you assume in the very premise of your argument the conclusion which is to be proved. The burden placed on the person making a claim or presenting an argument is to provide evidence on the basis of which the claim or conclusion can be seen to be true. Thus, the fallacy of begging the question attempts to get around the whole argumentation process. It may appear to be an argument but in fact it isn't. The reason it's not is that it fails to provide evidence in support of one's claim. If you say, "Jack doesn't tell the truth, so this makes him a liar," you have merely restated the claim in a different way. The two assertions differ from each other only verbally, not in terms of their content, so the very point that needs to be proven is assumed to be true, without any substantiation offered in its support (McInerny 2005, pp. 109–10).

Here's a joke where the question is begged:

A guy had been feeling down for so long that he finally decided to seek the aid of a psychiatrist. He went to the psychiatrist's office, lay on the couch, spilled his guts, then waited for the profound wisdom of the psychiatrist. The psychiatrist asked him a few questions, took some notes, then sat thinking in silence for a few minutes with a puzzled look on his face. Suddenly he looked up with an expression of delight and said, "Um, I think your problem is low self-esteem. It's very common among losers."

Under the guise of having figured out the patient's problem, the psychiatrist has basically begged the question. He reasons that the patient has low self-esteem because he is a loser and losers have low self-esteem. Thus, telling the patient that he is a loser doesn't add anything to the evidence that he has low self-esteem, and this makes the statement, "It's very common among losers," a gratuitous thing to say. Moreover, the question is begged since no real evidence has been provided by the psychiatrist in support of his claim that the patient has low self-esteem.

The fallacy of begging the question also comes in a broader version. Here, rather than making a circular argument, the person simply assumes what needs to be proven:

A minister, a priest, and a rabbi were playing poker when the police raided the game. Turning to the minister, the lead police officer said, "Reverend Allworthy, were you gambling?" Turning his eyes to heaven, the minister whispered, "Lord, forgive me for what I am about to do," then replied to the officer's question, "No, I was not gambling." Then the officer asked the priest, "Father Murphy, were you gambling?" Again, after an appeal to heaven, the priest replied, "No, I was not gambling." Turning to the rabbi, the officer again asked, "Rabbi Goldman, were you gambling?" Shrugging his shoulders, the rabbi replied, "With whom?"

This is an especially clever example of question begging because it can be taken in two different ways: On the one hand, the police officer is begging the question because he assumes that it is possible for Rabbi Goldman to have been gambling. But, as the rabbi points out, on the basis of his two colleagues' testimony, this assumption is no longer relevant. So, as the rabbi clearly recognized, the proper response to the police officer's question is not a straight "yes" or "no" since this would concede the police officer's assumption. Instead, the proper response is to point out that the police officer is begging the question: Rabbi Goldman can't be gambling because he has no one with whom to gamble, and gambling requires at least two participants.

But there's another way to take the joke: We know that the minister and the priest were lying when they denied that they were gambling. Thus, their denials gave the rabbi the perfect out: "How could I have been gambling if these two guys weren't gambling?" So the rabbi's response "With whom?" begs the question because his colleagues' denials of having gambled, and his desire (which is self-serving) not to reveal that they were gambling, leaves him no choice but to suggest that the matter is already settled. There is no need to provide evidence that he was not gambling. In contrast to the minister and priest who deny the gambling charge, the rabbi equivocates by responding to the police officer's question with another question. Begging the question, then, is a form of equivocation.

Here's another example:

> **An angry wife met her husband at the door. There was alcohol on his breath and lipstick on his cheek. "I assume," she said, "that there is a very good reason for you to come waltzing in at five o'clock in the morning?" "There sure is," he replied, "I haven't had breakfast."**

Of course, the wife's assumption that he has a good reason for coming home at five o'clock in the morning betrays a note of sarcasm. She does not really think that he has a very good reason for his behavior. But, in any case, he begs the question with an evasive response: he draws attention to a contextual factor (it's time for breakfast) that has nothing really to do with the real reason why he is coming in at five o'clock in the morning.

Here's another example:

> **Alice frowned at the man who, crouched on one knee, was proposing to her. "I'm sorry, Jack," she said, "I just can't marry you." "Why?" he asked. "Is there someone else?" The frown deepened. "Oh, Jack ... there must be."**

This seems like a rather benign case of begging the question, but begging the question can be an especially pernicious fallacy because persons who commit it usually try to give others the impression that they have good and solid reasons for what they are claiming. Sometimes, they disguise the fact that they are begging the question through evasions, and sometimes their evasions are so skillfully presented that we fail to recognize that the question itself has been begged. This means that this fallacy can be more difficult to detect than some of the others. However, one clue to keep an eye out for is unnecessary repetition. If someone repeats himself, hoping that by doing so his point will become more compelling, there's a good chance that he is begging the question. Raising one's voice is another clue. Both are quite common in political speeches, but they can happen in any setting where someone is trying to persuade or convince others but is unable to offer much if any grounds for the belief or claim being made.

Two Wrongs

A third fallacy of assumption is the two wrongs fallacy. It involves the claim that two wrongs make a right. That the very claim that two wrongs make a right is fallacious seems pretty obvious. After all, two wrongs simply make two wrongs. Why, then, would anyone think otherwise, making it necessary for those interested in critical thinking to have to say that two wrongs *don't* make a right? The most likely reason why someone might think that two wrongs could make a right is that the fallacy is typically stated in this way: "It's o.k. to do _____ because _____ already has been done." A common example is justifying our action on the grounds that we are merely respond-ing to what someone did to us: "He did this to me, and it was wrong for him to do so, so I'm fully justified in doing this to him." This justification is often used by groups, ranging from families to nations, who have been mistreated or ill-used in the past.

The reasoning behind the two wrongs fallacy is based on the assumption that precedent alone justifies future action. This was done to us (or me), so I have the right to do this to them (or her). But, in fact, precedent in and of itself does not provide sufficient justification for any action, and the fact that an act has been performed by others is of historical interest only. In deciding on the appropriateness of the action that is yet to take place and is intended as a response to the earlier action, we need to concentrate instead on the nature of the act itself (McInerny 2005, pp. 113–14).

Here's a joke that illustrates the two wrongs fallacy:

> **A big-city lawyer was representing the railroad in a lawsuit filed by an old rancher. The rancher's prize bull was missing from the section of his land where the railroad passed, and the rancher only wanted to be paid the fair value of the bull. Before the trial began, the lawyer cornered the rancher as**

> he was entering the county court house and tried to convince him to settle out of court. The lawyer did his best selling job, and finally the rancher agreed to take half of what he was originally asking for. After the rancher signed the release and took the check, the lawyer began to gloat over his success in getting the rancher to settle. "You know, I hate to tell you this, old man, but I put one over on you in there. I couldn't have won the case. The engineer was asleep and the fireman was in the caboose when the train went through your property that morning. I didn't have one witness to put on the stand. I bluffed you!" The old rancher replied, "Well, I'll tell you, young feller, I was a little worried about winning the case myself. Then, this morning, that darned bull returned home."

The lawyer thinks he's put one over on the rancher, but the rancher has actually put a bigger one over on the lawyer. Because the lawyer gloats (and lawyers aren't liked much anyway), we're glad that the rancher comes out on top.

What makes this joke interesting from a critical thinking point of view, though, is that we might be tempted to say, "Well, in this case, both wrongs *did* make a right. The lawyer did the rancher a wrong, but the rancher's wrong made everything come out right." Yet, that's not really true. There was a third party involved – the railroad company – which had to pay the rancher for half of what the bull was worth, and the judge and other court officials had a justifiable grievance because they had to waste time on a case that could have been dismissed if the rancher had come to court that morning and informed them that the bull had returned unharmed. We might not feel any pity for the company or the court, but they, too, were wronged, so, in this case, two wrongs made more wrong. Also, the truth itself was the victim of what the two men did. So, even if we may not be concerned about the company and the court, we should be concerned that truth was sacrificed to expedience by what the two men did.

The "two wrongs make a right fallacy" seems to begin in childhood. Among kids, it's pretty customary for one kid to defend hitting another kid because "he hit me first." This way of thinking, though, can last a long time, as this joke suggests:

> At a funeral, a guy punches the deceased in the nose. When another mourner asked, "Why in the world did you do that?" the guy replied, "Because he hit me first."

An obvious problem with this fallacy is that it can become an ongoing process with escalating damage. We see this in the political arena: "They started the dirty tricks, so we had to respond in kind. After all, we couldn't let them have this advantage over us." But all social groups – families, ethnicities, athletic teams, business competitors, etc. – have used it. Because it's so common, it's important to see that it is called a fallacy not just because it is illogical but also because there are better ways (both morally and prudentially) for persons who have been wronged to respond, and there are ways for those who have wronged others to respond (making a sincere apology, making reparations, etc.) which are preferable to waiting for the other to counter-attack.

However, there are situations where the wronged person doesn't want to counter-attack, but *does* want the offender to suffer for the harm that was done. In some cases, a third party steps in and sets the terms on how the offender will be made to suffer. Consider the case of Roy E. Frankhouser, who called himself a chaplain to the Ku Klux Klan. He harassed a woman by taking photographs of his victim through her office window, broadcasting images of an explosion destroying her office, making threatening phone calls, and distributing threatening fliers. The victim, a social worker whose job was to assist people filing discrimination complaints, was so fearful that she left her job and her home and repeatedly moved from one residence to another. The court imposed punishment for the wrongs he committed against her included submitting written copies of an apology to a major newspaper, performing community service, making efforts to promote anti-discrimination campaigns, and contributing a percentage of his salary to the victim and her daughter (Lazare 2004, p. 62).

Some people think that it's enough for the wrongdoer to make a sincere apology, but this is not necessarily the case: the victim's need for restoration of self-respect may be met by exercising the power (legal) to make the offender suffer. Another need that is satisfied is the need to believe that important values are in fact shared and that the offender feels bound by the social contract (Lazare 2004, p. 63). What's important to keep in mind is that there's a difference between requiring the offender to suffer and committing a retaliatory offense against the offender as a way of "getting even."

The Straw Man

A fourth fallacy of assumption is the straw man fallacy. If, in responding to someone else's argument, you deliberately distort it so as to weaken it, you commit the straw man fallacy. In the form in which you represent the other person's argument, it is easy to refute. That's why it's called a straw man. A straw man, after all, is an easy pushover. There's a difference, though, between committing this fallacy and making an honest mistake in interpreting what the other person has argued. Some arguments are complex and are not easy to grasp and sometimes our effort to restate the other person's argument requires modification or correction. But the commission of the straw man argument is a dishonest mistake because it involves the deliberate distortion of the other person's argument (McInerny 2005, p. 112). In effect, you want to make the other person look ridiculous and want those who are listening to the argument to say about your opponent's argument, "How could anyone possibly believe that?" So the straw man is an exercise in bad faith, as it often has an ad hominem intent.

This fallacy is often used in politics because the one who uses it not only wants to make the other person's argument look bad but also wants the other person to look bad. Other people may not necessarily care about the issues that are being argued about but they do care whether the candidate is thoughtful and intelligent. If you can make the other candidate's argument appear ridiculous, you have also raised doubts in the minds of others as to the intelligence of the person who allegedly thinks this way.

Because straw man jokes are difficult to find, we will repeat a joke that we presented in chapter 2 in our discussion of the appeal to inappropriate authority. It's not strictly a straw man joke, but it does illustrate the bad faith that lies behind this fallacy:

> **A guy goes into a bar, approaches the bartender, and says, "I've been working on a top secret project on molecular genetics for the past five years and I've just got to talk to someone about it." The bartender says, "Wait a minute. Before we talk about that, just answer a few questions. When a deer defecates, why does it come out like little pellets?" The guy doesn't know. The bartender then asks, "Why is it that when a dog poops, it lands on the ground and looks like a coiled rope?' The guy, again, says, "I don't have any idea." The bartender then says, "You don't know crap and you want to talk about molecular genetics?"**

We assume that the guy who comes into the bar knows a lot about molecular genetics. After all, he's been researching the subject for five years. It's also a fair assumption that the bartender doesn't know anything about molecular genetics and doesn't have any interest in the topic. So he brings up a topic that he *has* studied – how animals defecate – and uses this knowledge as a ploy to avoid having to discuss molecular genetics. In effect, he treats the other guy's knowledge as of lesser significance than his own, and demeans the guy in the process. We might add that he uses the fallacy of equivocation – the word "crap" can mean defecation but it can also mean nonsense or useless knowledge – to imply that the guy isn't capable of discussing anything as sophisticated as molecular genetics. We know, of course, that the bartender resorts to this ploy because he himself doesn't know "crap" about molecular genetics and other sophisticated topics.

As we noted in chapter 2, Michael Griffin, NASA's administrator, claimed that global warming is not a problem because there's no evidence that today's climate is optimal. In April 2008, Vice-President Richard Cheney said that there is clear evidence of global warming, adding with a laugh, "I call it spring." Like Griffin, Cheney minimized the potential seriousness of global warming, but used a different approach. As we saw, Griffin said that assuming this is a problem is to assume that the earth's climate today is the optimal one. We suggested that this was an appeal to ignorance. Cheney's quip is a case of the straw man fallacy because he trivializes the argument, based on scientific evidence, that the earth is undergoing climate changes (evidence that Griffin grants but questions the related claim that these changes are potentially catastrophic). In addition, there is an ad hominem tone to Cheney's quip as he holds those who advance global warming arguments up to ridicule.

Also, in making a joke ("I call it spring") Cheney uses laughter as a diversionary tactic (see McInerny 2005, pp. 122–3). We think this is a version of the straw man fallacy as it implies that the other person's argument is not worth taking seriously. In his essay on "The True Harvard," William James tells about a Canadian student in one of his classes, "a man with a high pitched voice, who couldn't fully agree with all the points of my philosophy. At a lecture one day, when I was in the full flood of my eloquence, his voice rose above mine, exclaiming: 'But, doctor, doctor! To be serious for a moment …' in so sincere a tone that the whole room burst out laughing" (James 1987b, p. 1126). We laugh, too, because the victim of this diversionary tactic tells the story in a self-deprecatory way, making light of his own eloquence. But it's doubtful that the other students would have burst out laughing if the professor had been an egotistical snob or if the victim of the Canadian student's gambit had been another student. In any case, McInerny points out: "To be sure, there are arguments that are comically inept and therefore deserving of laughter. But even in those cases it is better, rather than dismissing an argument with easy ridicule, to take the time to show how and why it fails as an argument" (p. 122).

The Slippery Slope

A fifth fallacy of assumption is the slippery slope fallacy. Genuine arguments usually involve a series of statements by the persons involved in the argument. This occurs because when we make an initial statement another person asks for clarification, asks whether we have considered so-and-so, and presents counter-arguments. The slippery slope fallacy occurs when we make a statement that is not very convincing then we compound the problem by following the statement up with an even weaker statement, until it becomes apparent to others that our argument is rather weak. This fallacy belongs among the fallacies of assumption because it often begins with an unwarranted assumption which the facts do not support but which we are reluctant to give up. As the facts against it escalate, we work doubly hard to hold onto it, and our argument gets increasingly desperate. On the other hand, this fallacy could also have been located among the fallacies of evidence, because it may begin with an unsupported claim for which we try to marshal evidence, but the evidence we offer becomes increasingly dubious or irrelevant.

Jokes that illustrate the slippery slope form of argumentation are difficult to come by, but there are quite a number of jokes in which one person's testimony to another gets increasingly problematic. A weak argument is not so much the issue, but a downward spiral is, and for this reason, the slippery slope fallacy and jokes have something in common. For example:

> A married couple was celebrating their fiftieth wedding anniversary. The husband asked his wife, "Darling, have you ever cheated on me?" "What a strange question to ask after all these years," she replied, "but if you must know, yes, I have cheated on you." The husband was saddened by this admission but wanted to know when. She replied, "Remember back when we were first married and you wanted to start a business but no bank would give you a loan? And remember how the bank president came to our house in person and signed the papers? Well ..." The husband was touched, "You mean, you slept with the president of the bank so that I could start up my business? That's the kindest thing anyone's ever done for me. Was this the only time?" "Well, if you must know, there was another time. Remember when you were 48 and you had a heart attack, and no surgeon would operate on you? And then Dr. Forrest came all the way up here to carry out that surgery himself, and performed the surgery gratis? Well ..." The husband was genuinely moved. "So you slept with Dr. Forrest to save my life. What

a wonderful woman you are! I assume these were the only times." She replied, "Well, if you really want to know, remember how a couple of years ago when you really wanted to be president of the golf club, but you were 52 votes short?"

The wife's explanation for the first two cases of infidelity sound plausible enough, but with the last one, the husband's belief in her basic faithfulness is pretty much in tatters. His response to the earlier acts, "You did this for me?" is rather hard to imagine following her revelation that she slept with 52 members of the golf club.

Here's a joke where the shoe is on the other foot:

A wife asked her husband, "Honey, if I died, would you remarry?" "After a considerable period of grieving, I guess I would. We all need companionship." "If I died and you remarried," the wife asked, "would she live in this house?" "We've spent a lot of money getting this house just the way we want it. I'm not going to get rid of my house. I guess she would, yes." "If I died and you remarried and she lived in this house," the wife continued, "would she sleep in our bed?" "Well, the bed is brand new, and it cost us over $2,000. It's going to last a long time, so I guess she would." "If I died and you remarried and she lived in this house and slept in our bed, would she use my golf clubs?" "Oh, no, certainly not," the husband replied, "She's left-handed."

Here we assume that the husband's answers are as hypothetical as the questions, until, that is, he answers the final question. Then we know that he has already been planning for the time when his wife is deceased.

A master at specious argumentation is the marriage broker. We met this fellow on an earlier occasion (in our discussion in chapter 3 of the denying the antecedent fallacy). Here's another illustration of how he reasons, also from Freud's book on jokes (Freud 1960, p. 71):

The marriage broker was defending the girl he had proposed against the young man's protests. "I don't care for the mother-in-law," said the latter, "She's a disagreeable, stupid person." "But, after all, you're not marrying the mother-in-law. What you want is her daughter." "Yes. But she's not young any longer, and she's not exactly a beauty." "No matter. If she's neither young nor beautiful she'll be all the more faithful to you." "And she hasn't much money." "Who's talking about money? Are you marrying money then? After all, it's a wife that you want." "But she's got a hunchback too." "Well, what *do* you want? Isn't she to have a single fault?"

This joke *is* a good example of the slippery slope fallacy because the broker and the young man are engaged in argumentation, and as the young man's counter arguments mount, the weakness of the marriage broker's case becomes increasingly apparent.

Freud's comments on this joke suggest that, despite his decision to enter medical school after majoring in philosophy as an undergraduate at the University of Vienna, he hadn't lost his love for critical reasoning. Here is what he says about the joke:

> What was really in question, then, was an unbeautiful girl, no longer young, with a scanty dowry and an unpleasant mother, who was moreover the victim of a serious deformity – not very inviting conditions for contracting a marriage. The marriage broker was able, in the case of each one of these defects, to point out how it would be possible to come to terms with it. He was then able to claim that the inexcusable hunchback was the single defect that every individual must be allowed to possess. There is the appearance of logic which is intended to conceal the faulty reasoning. Clearly the girl had a number of defects – several that might be overlooked and one that was impossible to disregard ... The broker behaved as though each separate defect was got rid of by his evasions, whereas in fact each one of them left a certain amount of depreciation behind which had to be added to the next one. He insisted on treating each defect in isolation and refused to add them up into the total. (p. 71)

In other words, the broker committed the slippery slope fallacy.

It's also noteworthy that Freud made the effort to analyze the broker's "faulty reasoning." Someone else might have said, "It's just a joke. I'm certainly not going to waste my mental capacities on a joke." But we think that this attitude is rather narrow-minded and shortsighted, especially in light of the fact that, although the marriage broker profession no longer exists, his methods are alive and well in other occupations. The mortgage broker comes especially to mind.

Conclusion

In these 3 chapters, we have presented 25 fallacies – 9 fallacies of relevance, 8 fallacies of evidence, and 5 fallacies of assumption. That's a lot of fallacies, and we'd be the first to acknowledge that it is unlikely that readers of this book will be able to remember them all, much less recall the category to which they have been assigned. What is more important, though, is that the sheer number of fallacies presented here may support or effect a certain mindset in the reader, one reflecting the recognition that many of the claims that people make are either groundless or so poorly expressed that it's little wonder that they fail to be convincing or even compelling. This very mind-set, however, may also produce a skeptical attitude toward the very search for objective truth, especially in a society in which the standards of truth and truth-telling are set incredibly low. We address these issues in the next chapter.

Good Point!

Certain crude and obvious cases of the comic seem to consist of little more than a shock of surprise: a pun is a sort of jack-in-the-box, popping from nowhere into our plodding thoughts. The liveliness of the interruption, and its futility, often please, and yet there is something inherently vulgar about it, perhaps because our train of thought cannot be very entertaining in itself when we are so glad to break in upon it with irrelevant nullities.

George Santayana

Bad Pun!!

A three-legged dog walked into a bar and said: "I'm looking for the man who shot my paw."

Anonymous

5 Critical Thinking and Objective Truth

We learn a great deal about how critical thinking can go wrong when we focus on fallacies of relevance, evidence, and assumptions. But we also learn in the process that the primary goal of critical thinking is to achieve or at least move closer to acquiring objective truth. In this chapter, therefore, we will discuss objective truth and several issues related to it, including the issues of proof, facts and values, collaborative critical thinking, and the case for a certain kind of radical skepticism.

Objective Truth

Thinking critically involves having good reasons for what we believe and being able to determine whether other persons have good reasons for what they believe. Believing something means considering it to be *true*: If I believe today is Tuesday, then I consider it to be true that today is Tuesday. It does not make sense to say, "I believe today is Tuesday, but I don't think that this is true." So, thinking critically means having good reasons for what we believe to be true, and this means that critical thinking is committed to true beliefs more than, say, to beliefs that are merely useful or comforting (although true beliefs may also be useful and comforting).

This commitment to truth has consequences. For one thing, it means that critical thinking is committed to identifying and pointing out that which is false. It also means that critical thinking aims to be objective. Consider this joke:

> A mathematician, a biologist and a physicist are sitting in a street café watching people going in and coming out of the house on the opposite side

of the street. First they see two people going into the house. Time passes. After a while they notice three persons coming out of the house. The physicist says, "The initial measurement wasn't accurate." The biologist says, "They must have reproduced." The mathematician says, "Now if exactly one person enters the house, it will be empty again."

Obviously, they can't all be right. Because their explanations are incompatible with each other, at least two must be false – in fact, the joke plays on the idea that if you think the biologist's explanation is dubious, the mathematician's is even more suspect. Thus, the joke illustrates the fact that truth is objective in ways that usefulness, for example, is not. Different things are useful to different people. It may be useful, for some unknown reason, for the mathematician to believe that you can have −1 person inside the house. But no matter how useful this belief may be, it doesn't make it objectively true.

By the same token, *not* believing something does not make it false. The truth or falsity of a statement does not depend on whether or not people believe it. Here's a supposedly true story about Niels Bohr, the Nobel Prize winning physicist: An American physicist once visited Bohr at his home and was surprised to find a horseshoe nailed to the wall above the front door. "Surely," his visitor said, "you don't believe that a horseshoe brings good luck!" Bohr replied, "Of course I don't believe in such nonsense. However, I've been told that a horseshoe brings you good luck whether you believe in it or not." More generally, we can say that the truth exists whether we believe in it or not. This is what it means to say that truth itself is objective.

This point is all too easily forgotten especially when people are deeply divided on an issue and/or the disagreement is one of longstanding. The mere fact that people disagree on an issue does not allow us to conclude that there is therefore no objective truth in this case. People disagree for all sorts of reasons, and it's important, therefore, to look at these reasons before we conclude that there's no objective truth involved and no point in trying to discover it. When we do examine these reasons, we invariably find that it simply isn't the case that there is no objective truth. After all, we might disagree simply because there isn't enough evidence available as yet to decide definitively one way or the other. But new evidence may come to light and, when it does, we will all recognize what was true all along and the disagreement itself will be laid to rest. For example, even though people once disagreed over whether the earth revolved around the sun or vice versa, the first was always objectively true. Here's an example:

> A guy was wandering around a fairground and he happened to see a fortune-teller's tent. With nothing better to do, he went inside and sat down. "Ah ..." said the fortune-teller as she gazed into her crystal ball. "I see you are the father of two children." "That's what *you* think," he replied, I'm the father of *three* children." The fortune-teller smiled and said, "That's what *you* think."

The fact that the two of them disagree does not mean that there is no objective truth. After all, they can't both be right. On the other hand, they could both be *wrong*. He could be the father of one child or, alternatively, the father of four or more children. If a person says that she has $10, this does not mean that she has $10 and no more. She could have $20 or $30, or even $1,000. This joke is also interesting because it assumes that there is an objective truth involved and wants us to believe that the fortune-teller knows what it is. However, she offers no evidence in support of her claim, relying instead on the mystique of the crystal ball.

Thus, the mere fact that people disagree should not discourage us from seeking the truth. Nor should it discourage us from thinking critically about the reasons people have for what they believe. In fact, disagreement can lead us to consider different points of view, to re-examine our own positions, and to refine the reasons we have for believing what we believe. This means that disagreements are a golden opportunity for thinking critically, and that the very fact that there is an objective truth (even though we do not yet know what it is) should dissuade us from taking the easy way out by saying, "Everyone's entitled to his or her opinion."

Here's a joke that illustrates what we've been saying here about objective truth:

> In a small town in Russia, people brought their complaints to the rabbi to settle their differences. One day, two men were before the rabbi. He listened to the first man and said, "You are right." He listened to the second man and said, "You are right." When the two men left, the rabbi's wife, who was listening from the next room, said to him, "You're supposed to be a judge! They can't both be right!" He thought for a moment, then replied, "You know what? You're right, too."

We're not told what the dispute itself was all about. It could have been over a factual question (such as who owns a piece of land) or a moral question (such as whether one man cheated the other man). But the rabbi refused or was unable to rule in favor of one or the other, so his wife was right to point out that, in the context of rendering a judgment, her husband had, in effect, abdicated his role as a judge. On the other hand, it is also possible that the rabbi should not have agreed with his wife that both men could not be right for, conceivably, they both had a rightful claim and, if so, the rabbi did not abdicate his role as a judge, appearances notwithstanding. But unless his agreement with his wife was merely prudential (e.g., he didn't want to have to argue with her), it's hard not to conclude that he's ill-equipped temperamentally to be a judge because he is unable to say anyone is wrong, which is something judges are required to do. The rabbi is not alone: we are not professional judges, but we too have a responsibility to distinguish true from false and right from wrong whether we're discussing science, ethics, politics, religion, morality, parenting, etc.

The Issue of Proof

The very affirmation that truth is objective raises an important problem, namely, the fact that it is often difficult to prove that a belief or claim is true. This being so, some people will say that a claim that cannot be proven cannot be justified and is therefore beyond the limits of critical thinking. This raises the question: How important is it to *prove* one's claim? We would say: Not very. Why? Although a mathematical statement (such as the Pythagorean theory) can be proven by logically deducing it from axioms, most statements about the everyday world cannot be proven in the same way. Here's a joke that illustrates the point:

> A quiet little man was brought before a judge. The judge looked down at the man and then at the charges against him and back at the little man. He could barely conceal his amazement. "Can you tell me in your own words what happened?" he asked the man. "I'm a mathematical logician dealing in the nature of proof." "Yes, go on," said the judge. "Well, I was at the library and I found the books I wanted and went to the desk to check them out. I was informed that my library card had expired and that I had to get a new one. So I went to the registration office and got in another line. They gave me a form to fill out so I filled it out and got back in line for my card." "And?' said the judge. "Well, the fellow at the desk asked me if I could prove that I'm a New York City resident. So I kicked him in the crotch."

This joke plays on the widely held perception that New Yorkers are combative (a hasty generalization?). Presumably, you can prove you're a New Yorker by kicking your questioner in the crotch. What's especially relevant to the issue of proof, though, is that this particular New Yorker is an expert on the nature of mathematical proof and would therefore know that he cannot *prove* that he is a New York City resident. Instead, the best he can do is to kick the other man in the crotch. Why this rather extreme way of convincing him? Wouldn't a driver's license prove it? Well, no, because it could be a fake. Also, some people who live in New York City do not have driver's licenses. They rely on public transportation, cabs, bicycles, and walking. What about credit cards? They would identify the man but not the fact that he is a resident of New York City. How about the phone book? But who carries around a phone book? So, in the absence of proof, kicking his questioner seemed to him to be as convincing as any other evidence he might offer in support of his claim to be a resident of New York City.

In the everyday world, it's alright that you cannot provide absolute proof for your beliefs and claims. Your evidence may not be absolutely conclusive, but if it is compelling, that's usually more than good enough. In such cases the right response to "but you can't *prove* it" is "true, but I *can* support it beyond any reasonable doubt." Critical thinking focuses on whether someone has *good* reasons for what he or she believes. When we think critically it's important to remember that good reasons come in degrees. Sometimes the reasons are absolutely conclusive; other times they are compelling but not conclusive; and sometimes they warrant a healthy amount of skepticism, such as in this joke:

> Three drunks are staggering down the street. One suddenly stops and says, "I'm the President of the United States!" His companions say, "Oh, yeah? Prove it!" and he quiets down. A few minutes later the second drunk stops and says, "I'm the King of England!" His companions say, "Oh, yeah? Prove it!" and he, too, quiets down. A few more minutes pass by and the third drunk shouts out, "I'm God!" His companions say, "Oh, yeah? Prove it!" He responds, "OK, I will." So he leads them into the next bar and staggers in. When the bartender sees him, he says, "Oh, God, you again."

Obviously, this "proof" is not enough. In fact, it relies on the fallacy of equivocation (presented in chapter 3 on fallacies of evidence) because "God" in this case is being used in two different ways: as referring to the deity and as an interjection or oath.

Other claims, however, do not call for so much skepticism. In fact, some claims are so obvious and well-supported that it would be unreasonable to doubt them (for example, that Canada geese fly south in the winter and that drowning your own babies is morally wrong) and the burden is therefore on those who raise doubts to show why it is reasonable to believe them. It is not enough for them to say vaguely, "But you can't *prove* that." What's at stake here is the limits that an absolute standard of proof places on critical thinking. We have many beliefs and make many claims that cannot be proven. These range from the mundane (where one lives) to the extremely important (global warming). The fact that we cannot prove these claims and beliefs does not mean that we cannot give good reasons on their behalf. The kick in the crotch was effective, but the mathematician's questioner would have been satisfied had he presented his driver's license.

Facts and Values

Many people draw a sharp distinction between "facts" and "values." Statements of fact, they say, can be objectively true but statements of values (such as whether something is good, beautiful, or right) cannot be objectively true. If this is correct, then critical thinking is limited to questions of fact and we cannot think critically about values. Some values, however, are as objective as facts. This does not mean, of course, that all values are objective for some are clearly subjective: some people believe that blue is the most beautiful color while others make the same claim for green, yellow, pink, purple, etc. It would be a mistake, however, to assume that all values are subjective. This becomes clear when we see how the distinction between facts and values often disappears. For example, the statement "It is wrong to drown babies" is a statement of value because it says that drowning babies is morally wrong. At the same time, it is a fact that drowning babies is wrong, and this is as clear and obvious as any other straightforward statement of fact. One could say that it's actually more obvious that it is wrong to drown babies than that the earth is round and not flat because, after all, the earth *looks* flat.

Two further points: first, even though it is obvious that it's wrong to drown babies, one can still argue in support of this fact. The problem in this case is not having too few (as is often the case) but having too many reasons, so many in fact that most people will find it puzzling when someone feels the need to enumerate the reasons why drowning babies is wrong.

The important point here, though, is that we *can* give reasons should any-one want to argue that there's *nothing* wrong with drowning babies or, per-haps more likely, contend that the belief that it is wrong to drown babies is merely a cultural value and not an objective truth.

Second, the fact that there are often extenuating circumstances when babies are drowned does not mean that the drowning of babies is not itself objec-tively wrong. We cited the case of Andrea Yates in chapter 2 in our discussion of the appeal to pity fallacy. A recent study of women in the United States who had killed their children found that three-quarters of them had received prior psychiatric care and half of them had been previously psychiatrically hospital-ized (Friedman, Hrouda, and Holden 2005). Mental illness of the mother is certainly an extenuating circumstance and is an important consideration when we discuss the sanctions imposed on these women by courts of law. These circumstances, however, do not challenge the objective truth that drowning babies is morally wrong. In fact, they actually support it.

Many jokes illustrate that there is no distinction between a fact and a value as far as objective truth is concerned. For example:

> **A client felt his legal bill was too high and asked his lawyer to itemize costs. The statement included this item: "Was walking down the street and saw you on the other side. Walked to the corner at the light, crossed the street and walked quickly to catch up with you. Got close and saw it wasn't you – $50.00."**

This joke depends on it being a fact that the lawyer acted unethically. Or take this joke:

> **A worried new mother went to the psychiatrist. "Doctor," she said, "Ever since I had the baby I can't sleep at night. When I'm in the next room, I have this dreadful fear that I won't hear the baby if he falls out of the crib. What should I do?" "That's easy," the doctor replied, "Just remove the carpet from the floor."**

This joke also depends on it being a fact that the doctor has said something morally wrong. If there were no objective truth in these two cases, the jokes would be rather pointless (or, to put it another way, no one would "get" the joke).

Here's an interesting example of how a "clean" version of a joke is actually more questionable from a moral point of view. Here's a version that does not claim to be "clean" (Tapper and Press 2000, pp. 178–9):

A respectable lady bought a parrot from a pet store, only to discover after bringing the bird home that it would say nothing but, "My name is Mary, and I'm a whore." Weeks of trying to teach the parrot other phrases proved hopeless. Furthermore, much to this respectable lady's embarrassment, the parrot dropped the same line at the most awkward moments. One day her parish priest dropped by for a visit and, sure enough, while he was there the parrot squawked out the only words it would say. The woman apologized to the priest, explaining that the parrot resisted all efforts at reformation. The priest offered to take the bird home for a visit with his own two parrots, as their repertoire consisted entirely of saying Hail Mary's while clutching rosaries. He was certain that his parrots would have a positive influence on the lady's bird. So he took her parrot home and put it in the cage with the other birds, and, sure enough, the first words out of her mouth were, "My name is Mary, and I'm a whore." Whereupon, one of the priest's parrots squawked to his companion, "Throw that rosary away! Our prayers have been answered!"

Here's a version of essentially the same joke as presented in a book of "good clean jokes" (Phillips 1998, p. 190).

A dignified old clergyman owned a parrot of whom he was exceedingly fond, but the bird had picked up an appalling vocabulary of cuss words from a previous owner and, after a series of embarrassing episodes, the clergyman decided he would have to kill his pet. A lady in his parish suggested a last ditch remedy. "I have a female parrot," she said, "who is an absolute saint. She sits quietly on her perch and says nothing but 'Let's pray.' Why don't you bring your parrot over and see if my own bird's good influence doesn't reform him." The clergyman said it was worth a trial, and the next night he arrived with his pet tucked under his arm. The bird took one look at the lady parrot and chirped, "Hi, toots, how about a little kiss?" "My prayers have been answered," said the lady parrot gleefully.

It seems unlikely that we are meant to assume that "Hi, toots, how about a little kiss?" is evidence that the clergyman's parrot, on seeing the lady parrot, had already begun to clean up his language. If so, the clean version of the joke would have us believe that a "dignified old clergyman" is planning to *kill* his parrot for rather innocuous language. "Hi, toots, how about a little kiss?" is so far from an "appalling vocabulary of cuss words" that the clergyman's plan to kill the parrot seems a gross overreaction. Furthermore, however "appalling" the parrot's vocabulary might be, does this give the clergyman the moral right to kill him? Thus, the other version makes more sense and this makes it more truthful. The distinction between fact and values collapses.

Here's a joke that presents some interesting challenges for thinking critically about values because it seems to violate one set of human values while upholding another set:

A small Midwestern manufacturing company, Anderson Nails, had been experiencing years of success and growth. Feeling that the company was ready to try for the big time, the founder and owner, Mr. Anderson, contracted a big Madison Avenue advertising agency to help him promote his product. Aiming to get the greatest possible exposure, the agency booked a full minute at the beginning of the Super Bowl's halftime show. Anderson was very excited about this, and invited all of his friends and relatives to his home for a big Super Bowl party. At the end of the first half, everybody drew closer to the TV, waiting to see the premiere of the commercial. It began with an aerial shot of the desert and then zoomed in on a walled city. As the camera slowly panned about the city, it became apparent that this was Jerusalem during the Roman occupation. A large hill on the horizon came into view and as the camera drew closer, three crosses became visible. The focus settled on a naked man in a crown of thorns, then moved in for an extreme close-up of his bleeding hands and the nails that held them to the cross. Clearly visible were the words MANUFACTURED BY ANDERSON NAILS. A subtitle appeared on the screen bearing the words, "Anderson Nails – The 'Expert's Choice.' " Mr. Anderson's guests were horrified. The party broke up before the end of the game. The next day he began to get phone calls from his oldest and most loyal customers, expressing their outrage and canceling their orders. By the end of the week, his sales were down to nothing. He called the president of the advertising agency to cancel his contract. When he explained the situation, the ad man was surprised and offered to run a new campaign at no charge. The new campaign was slated to begin in a few weeks' time. This time, Anderson nervously watched the commercial alone in the privacy of his office. It began the same way as before, with an aerial view of Jerusalem. The camera finally settled on two Roman soldiers drinking wine at a table by a marketplace. Hearing a disturbance nearby, they looked up from their drinks in time to see a naked man with bleeding hands and feet being pursued by a group of soldiers. The first soldier looked at his companion, smiled knowingly, and said, "I bet they didn't use Anderson Nails."

One of the things that make this an especially interesting joke from the perspective of values is that the issue of offense is built into the joke itself.

Mr. Anderson's guests take serious offense at the commercial and his customers, no less offended, cancel their orders. They are reacting to the very idea that anyone would exploit the crucifixion of Jesus for commercial gain. What about the readers of this joke? Do we respond as they responded, viewing the joke itself as insensitive to the suffering of a fellow human being? Or do we view it as a lampoon of the Madison Avenue advertising industry and of *its* insensitivity to the values and tastes of middle America? Minimally, the joke does not allow us, it would seem, to say that values are outside the purview of critical thinking, that the issues it raises are matters merely of subjective preference or taste.

We conclude, therefore, that there can be objective truths when it comes to values, and that it is worthwhile to think critically about these. To be sure, someone might object that searching for the objective truth in this regard can make one close-minded and intolerant of alternative viewpoints. This *is* a possibility. At the same time, we shouldn't be so open-minded that our brains fall out (as Bertrand Russell once remarked). Instead, the real question is whether one's tolerance or intolerance is justified. Whether one's tolerance is justified is an important, valid question that we can and should attempt to answer, so we begin with the assumption that it has an objectively true answer that we can look into. If it turns out that the question does *not* have an objectively true answer then we hope that our investigation will show *that* too, since that's how we find out that we're wrong about this. If we had instead assumed the opposite, that this question has no objectively true answer, then there would be no point in even asking the question and no reason to look into it further. On that assumption, we would have blocked ourselves from ever learning that we were wrong. This shows how believing that there is no objective truth as far as values are concerned leads to its own kind of intolerance: if there is no objective truth, then there is no reason to think that I might be wrong and you might be right, and we would become prisoners of our own biases and prejudices.

Thinking Together

Critical thinking is often a solitary act. We work out our beliefs pretty much on our own. Or we face a situation that calls for thinking critically and we rely on ourselves to figure it out or solve it. But critical thinking can also be done collaboratively and there are often benefits to doing it this way. This is one reason why there are college courses in critical reasoning that often include class discussion. There are times when two or more persons simply have to think about an issue together because the answer depends on the input that each of them is uniquely able to provide. There are also times when, as we noted in our discussion in chapter 2 on the appeal to inappropriate authority, we need to consult with someone who has the knowledge that we need in order to think critically about a situation or issue. Consider this joke:

> Five guys staggered out of the bar and headed down the street at about one o'clock in the morning. Laughing and singing loudly, they walked up to a two-story home. One of them managed to make it to the door and pounded on the doorbell. A light came on in an upstairs window. The spokesman for the group yelled up, "Is this where Mr. John Smith lives?" "Yes, it is. What do you want?" "Are you Mrs. Smith?" "Yes, I am. What do you want?" "Could you come down here and identify your husband so the rest of us can go home?"

In their present state of intoxication, the five guys can't identify one another, so they ask someone else to help them solve their problem. At least they recognize that they need some outside help, and seeking outside help will continue until all five are safely home in bed.

Here's a joke that illustrates how a couple of individuals engage together in effective critical thinking, supporting the idea that sometimes two minds are better than one:

> Two beggars are sitting on a park bench in Mexico City. One is holding a crucifix and the other a Star of David. Both are holding hats to collect contributions. People walk by and lift their noses at the beggar with the Star of David, and then drop money in the hat held by the beggar with the crucifix. Soon the hat of the beggar with the crucifix is filled, and the hat of the beggar with the Star of David is still empty. A priest watches and then approaches the two beggars. He turns to the beggar with the Star of David and says, "Young man, don't you realize that this is a Catholic country? You'll never get any contributions in this country holding a Star of David." The beggar with the Star of David turns to the beggar with the cross and says, "Moishe, can you imagine, this guy is trying to tell us how to run our business?"

This joke is clever because the passersby assume that the beggar with the crucifix is Catholic and the beggar with the Star of David is Jewish, so they snub the beggar they believe to be Jewish and put their money in the hat of the beggar they assume is Catholic. But both are Jewish (the name "Moishe" makes that clear) and they know that people will be more inclined to put money in the hat of the beggar with the crucifix if the beggar with the Star of David is sitting next to him than if he were sitting all by himself. Of course, it's possible that one of the two beggars thought this scheme up and the other beggar simply went along with it, so this may not be a perfect example of collaborative critical thinking. Even so, the execution of the scheme requires two beggars, and the two of them together are doing a better job of thinking than the priest, who thinks, erroneously, that he is thinking more critically than they are. We can imagine that if a group of priests had passed by, they may well have figured out what was going on. Why? Because, collectively, they would have been able to take more adequate account of the evidence that was presented to them: the fact that the two beggars were sitting together, the fact that they were both holding religious symbols, and that they both probably looked Jewish.

Interestingly enough, when one of us told this joke to a colleague, he laughed and said, "So a Jew and a Protestant put one over on the Catholics!" In effect, the colleague didn't really "get" the joke, and this very fact makes the point that critical thinking done collaboratively can often – though certainly not always – be superior to critical thinking done alone.

There are, of course, different ways in which critical thinking is done on a collaborative basis. Sometimes, two or more persons engage in critical thinking simultaneously. This can happen, for example, when a committee meets to discuss a problem confronting the organization. All the committee members are expected to think about the problem and share their ideas on how the problem might be addressed. Other times, one person gets the thinking process underway and another person builds on what this person has initiated. This more sequential approach often occurs in scientific research. Consider this example:

> A guy goes into a bar with a German shepherd dog and sits down at the counter. The bartender says, "You can't bring that German shepherd in here! Dogs ain't allowed!" The guy replies, "But this is a Seeing Eye dog." The bartender says, "Well, in that case, I guess it can stay." After awhile the guy and the German shepherd get up to leave. As they are heading out the door, another guy with a Chihuahua is coming in, and the first guy says, "The bartender won't like you bringing a dog in here, but if you tell him it's a Seeing Eye dog, maybe he'll let you stay." The second guy looks dubiously at his tiny Chihuahua, thinks a few seconds, thanks the guy, and goes in.

The bartender says, "Hey! You can't bring that Chihuahua in here!" The man stares straight ahead and exclaims, "What! They sold me a Chihuahua?!"

In this case, the first guy does some thinking, passes it along to the second guy, and the second guy, realizing that his situation is a bit more complicated than that of the first guy, improvises on what the first guy did. Like the joke about the two Jewish beggars, their ruse raises some ethical questions that bring to mind the preceding discussion of facts and values. But our point here is that critical thinking may be sequential, with one person building on and modifying the thinking of another person. This point brings us to a final issue, namely, the case for a kind of radical skepticism.

Critical Thinking and Radical Skepticism

Harry Frankfurt, emeritus philosophy professor at Princeton University, made quite a stir several years ago with his book *On Bullshit* (2005). He began with the following observation:

> One of the most salient features of our culture is that there is so much bullshit. Everyone knows this. Each of us contributes his share. But we tend to take the situation for granted. Most people are rather confident of their ability to recognize bullshit and to avoid being taken in by it. So the phenomenon has not aroused much deliberate concern, nor attracted much sustained inquiry. In consequence, we have no clear understanding of what bullshit is, why there is so much of it, or what functions it serves. (p. 1)

In these sentences, Frankfurt, in effect, issues a call for critical thinking about bullshit. The aim of his book is to give a rough account of what bullshit is and is not.

Reviewers of the book point out that it evolved out of an essay Frankfurt wrote on the subject in 1986, which suggests that bullshit is nothing new. In fact, thirteen years before Frankfurt wrote the 1986 essay, Arthur Herzog brought attention to the phenomenon of bullshit in his book *The B. S. Factor* (1973). Interestingly enough, both conclude their books with a discussion of skepticism. Frankfurt suggests that the deeper sources of the contemporary proliferation of bullshit lie in "various forms of skepticism which deny that we can have any reliable access to an objective reality, and which therefore reject the possibility of knowing how things truly are" (p. 64). He adds that these "antirealist" doctrines "undermine confidence in the value of disinterested efforts to determine what is true and what is false, and even in the intelligibility of the notion of objective inquiry" (p. 65). Thus, these forms of skepticism go too far.

On the other hand, Herzog calls for a kind of "radical skepticism" that is suspicious of the way that words are used (equivocation?), especially by public figures, and he provides an account of how a person like himself becomes a radical skeptic. In his view and experience, the radical skeptic is unlikely to emerge full-blown. Instead, one is likely to have gone through three identifiable stages.

The first, or detective, phase begins as a result of experience, error, and disappointment. Faced with endless contradictions in ideas, people, and things, one becomes impatient and frustrated. One sets out on a quest to discover what is true and what is false and thinks that if this can be done, one can find peace of mind in truth and certainty. So, one considers all arguments and doctrines with the idea of learning the right way to go about it. What one discovers, though, is that no serious truths are valid because for every good argument there is an equally good counterargument (pp. 213–14). Most people quit at this point. They say, in effect, that it's all a matter of opinion, and that one person's opinion is no better – but no worse – than another person's opinion.

But the fledgling radical skeptic presses on, moving into the second phase. Here one develops the habit and strategy of suspending judgment altogether. All possibilities seem equally open (or closed) and no one system of values is any better (or worse) than any of the others. Words, especially, appear to be very unreliable agents for defining reality. At best, they describe it, but, even then, very poorly. In this phase, in near despair, one "almost succumbs to the condition of quietude and immobility" (p. 214).

But there is something nagging inside that prompts the radical skeptic to press further. These are the nagging contradictions that prompted the truth-trek in the very beginning. One enters the third phase of the journey and sees one's quest in a new light precisely because one recognizes the dilemma in which one finds oneself: on the one hand, the truth can't exist; on the other hand, one lives out one's whole life acting as if some things were true, as when one walks across a floor without asking whether it will hold oneself up. Of course, one tells oneself, no truth is involved in the floor, merely confidence, which is a summing up of previous experience. But the question gets harder when beliefs are involved because then one does think that some things are more probable than others, and one is forced to act as though some things are truer than others, even though nothing is finally true. But how does one establish the strength of the probability? Through reading the evidence, yes, but in a more general sense, from what happens as a result of one's own actions (pp. 214–15).

At this point, one knows that one must act *as though* one's assumptions were valid, without being really sure and always reserving the right to change one's mind. Furthermore, one must act wholeheartedly, because only then is it possible to give one's assumptions a serious test by bringing one's experiments to the point of actual results, which can then be seen and measured. In gauging the results, one remains the questioner, the doubter, looking at the answers in as practical a way as one can, and as much as possible in terms of one's everyday experience (p. 215). One's doubt, therefore, is not the same as indecision and paralysis; it causes one to *act*.

One acts, however, not blindly – "watch out," "take your time," "be careful," one tells oneself – but as one's analysis leads. Specifically, one seeks to cut through, with one's questions and sense of things, the propaganda and self-serving syllogisms that dominate the mind of our time. One has a feeling for limits and a desire to avoid futile controversy. One's hatred of either/or reasoning, one's dialectical disposition to juxtapose contradictory argu ments, helps one skirt the sham polemics and empty wars that rage around oneself. One's wariness of abstract logic spares one from being stuck in time and mental space. Above all, one's avoidance of ideas based on fixed principles of mind and human nature keep one open to new experience (p. 216).

Critical Thinking is Lifelong

Herzog's "radical skepticism" is very different from the skepticism that Frankfurt identifies – and challenges – in his book. It is a skepticism that does not believe there can be no objective truth, that does not accept the notion that everyone's opinion is as good as another's, and that does not succumb to indecision and paralysis as far as searching for what is sound, reliable, and defensible is concerned. Herzog calls this individual a radical skeptic, but it may be more accurate to say that he or she is an intrepid inquirer, with an inquiring mind that truly wants to know and is not easily discouraged in the search for what is true and right. Like the fellow in the following joke:

> A philosophy student went out on his first date with a classmate and took her to a nice restaurant. They sat quietly for awhile until he finally spoke, "Do you like philosophy?" She replied, "No, I really don't." He mused for a awhile, then asked, "Do you have a brother?" "No." He thought some more, "If you had a brother, do you think he would like philosophy?"

Things are not going well, but fortunately he's had a class in critical thinking and knows what's happening, so he changes the subject: "How's school going?" She says fine, then tells about what happened that morning in her US government class: They were waiting for class to begin when a student sitting nearby discovered that his wallet was missing. They looked under their chairs but didn't find it. So, finally, the student went up to the podium and said to the rest of the class, "I'm sorry to bother you, but I seem to have lost my wallet, and it had $100 in it. I'll give $25 to anyone who finds and returns it." Then, some guy on the other side of the classroom yelled out, "I'll give $50." Unknowingly, she had presented her date a golden opportunity to show what he could do. They had a stimulating discussion about facts and values and the relevance of what happened in class to the subject of the course.

By the time dessert was served, she was so impressed with the practical intelligence of her date that when he asked if she would like to go out with him again, she not only accepted his invitation, but added, "I like the way you think." He resisted the temptation to point out the inconsistency in disliking philosophy but liking the way a philosopher thinks, and this very resistance indicated that he had learned to take the context into account. To follow up on his earlier line of questioning, however, he *did* ask her if she had a sister, to which she replied, "No, but I have a dog, and he likes philosophy."

Our philosopher responded, "Then your dog would be interested in the fact that as a young physiology professor at Harvard, William James was actively engaged in animal research." He went on to tell her about how, in *The Principles of Psychology* (1950), James described his use of vivisection methods to explore the frog's nervous system and also discussed contemporary research on the brains of lizards, pigeons, doves, monkeys, and dogs (pp. 14–19). Then, in 1875, he wrote a short piece defending vivisection. He made his sympathies for lab animals very clear, noting, for example, that "a dog strapped on a board and howling at his executioners, or still worse, poisoned with curara, which leaves him paralyzed but sentient, is, to his own consciousness, literally in a sort of hell," and called for compassion among researchers, and thought that the day might be near when all that could be learned from vivisection would have been learned. On the other hand, he noted that the entire science of physiology "is based, immediately or remotely, upon vivisection evidence" so "to taboo vivisection is then the same thing as to give up seeking after knowledge of physiology." He added that if the dog understood the purposes of the research, "and if he were a heroic dog, he would religiously acquiesce in his own sacrifice" (Richardson 2006, p. 163).

In 1909, nearly thirty-five years after he conducted his own experiments, James wrote a letter to the secretary of the Vivisection Reform Society that was published in the *New York Evening Post* (Myers 1986, p. 433). After declining the invitation to become a vice-president of the society on the grounds that he didn't have the organizational skills required of someone in that office and that he had made it a principle not to let his name appear where he is not engaged in practical work, he went on to state his current views on the subject of vivisection. He said that he found much of the talk against vivisection to be as "idiotic" as the talk in its defense, but he indicated that he supported the society's aim to regulate (not abolish) the practice on ethical grounds. The defenders of vivisection object to any regulation whatsoever, contending that "it is *no one's business* what happens to an animal, so long as the individual who is handling it can plead that to increase *science* is his aim." In his view, this contention flatly contradicts "the best conscience of our time" for the "rights of the helpless, even though they be brutes, must be protected by those who have superior power." He added (Myers 1986, pp. 433–4):

> The public demand for regulation rests on a perfectly sound ethical principle, the denial of which by the scientists speaks ill for either their moral sense or their political ability. So long as the physiologists disdain corporate responsibility, formulate no code of vivisection ethics for laboratories to post up and enforce, appoint no censors, pass no votes of condemnation or exclusion, propose of themselves no law, so long must the anti-vivisectionist agitation, with all its expansiveness, idiocy, bad temper, untruth, and vexation continue as the only possible means of bringing home to the experimenter the fact that the sufferings of his animals *are* somebody else's business as well as his own.

In this letter James makes no reference to the heroism of the dog. Instead, he claims that it is not enough for the researcher to appeal to scientific objectives alone, but there are also ethical issues involved, i.e., the protection of the rights of the helpless by those who have superior power.

"Here," the philosophy student said to his companion, "We have an example of how a thoughtful person's thinking about an issue matured over the years." And this, of course, reminded him of a joke:

> A rabbit escaped from the research laboratory where he had been born and bred. On his first taste of freedom, he met a group of wild rabbits frolicking in a field. "Hi," he said, introducing himself, "I've escaped from the laboratory and I've never been outside before. What do you rabbits do all day?" "See that field over there?" they replied, "It's full of plump, juicy carrots. Care to try some?" So they all went off and ate some carrots. "That was great," said the escaped rabbit afterwards. "What else do you do?" "See that field over there?" they said, "It's full of fat lettuces. Care to try some?" So they all went off and devoured the lettuces. "This is wonderful," said the escaped rabbit, "I really love it out here in the wild." "So are you going to stay with us?" they asked. "I'd really like to," he answered, "but I've got to get back to the laboratory. I'm dying for a cigarette."

The student didn't need to state the obvious: sometimes jokes make a lot of sense.

Good Point!

The most common kind of joke is that in which we expect one
thing and another is said. Here our own disappointed expectation
makes us laugh. But if something ambiguous is thrown in too, the
effect of the joke is heightened.

Cicero

Good Limerick!!

A bather whose clothing was strewed
By winds, that left her quite nude,
   Saw a man come along,
   And unless I am wrong,
You expected this line to be rude.

Anonymous

References

Baden-Powell, Robert (2004). *Scouting for Boys*. Elleke Boehmer (ed.). Oxford: Oxford University Press.

Beers, Mark H. (2003). *The Merck Manual of Medical Information*. 2nd edition. New York: Pocket Books.

Bergson, Henri (1912). *Laughter: An Essay on the Meaning of the Comic*. Cloudesley Brereton and Fred Rothwell (trans.). New York: The Macmillan Company. Originally published in 1900.

Boy Scouts of America National Council (1948). *Handbook for Boys*. Location and publisher not identified.

Brooks, David (2007). Truck Stop Confidential. *The New York Times*, August 14.

Cathcart, Thomas and Daniel Klien (2007). *Plato and a Platypus Walk Into a Bar…: Understanding Philosophy through Jokes*. New York: Harry N. Abrams, Inc.

Cohen, Ted (1999). *Jokes: Philosophical Thoughts on Joking Matters*. Chicago: University of Chicago Press.

Davies, Christie (1998). *Jokes and Their Relation to Society*. Berlin: Mouton de Gruyter.

Dworkin, Gerald (1988). *The Theory and Practice of Autonomy*. Cambridge: Cambridge University Press.

Engle, Meagan (2007). More Time Given for Endangering Son. *The Cincinnati Post*, April 28.

Frankfurt, Harry G. (2005). *On Bullshit*. Princeton, NJ: Princeton University Press.

Freud, Sigmund (1960). *Jokes and Their Relation to the Unconscious*. James Strachey (trans.). New York: W. W. Norton & Company. Originally published in 1905.

Friedman, S. Hatters, Hrouda, D. L., and Holden, C. E. (2005). Child Murder Committed by Severely Mentally Ill Mothers: An Examination of Mothers Found Not Guilty by Reason of Insanity, *Journal of Forensic Sciences* 50: 1466–71.

Geller, Jeffrey L. and Harris, Maxine (1994). *Women of the Asylum: Voices from behind the Walls (1840–1945)*. New York: Doubleday.

Herzog, Arthur (1973). *The B. S. Factor*. New York: Simon and Schuster.

Holt, Jim (2008). *Stop Me If You've Heard This: A History and Philosophy of Jokes.* New York: W. W. Norton & Company.

James, William (1950). *The Principles of Psychology*, vol. 1. New York: Dover Publications. Originally published in 1890.

James, William (1987a). *Pragmatism: A New Name for Some Old Ways of Thinking.* In William James, *Writings 1902–1910* (pp. 479–624). Bruce Kuklick (ed.). New York: The Library of America.

James, William (1987b). The True Harvard. In William James, *Writings 1902–1910* (pp. 1126–9). Bruce Kuklick (ed.). New York: The Library of America.

Kaplan, Abraham (1964). *The Conduct of Inquiry.* San Francisco: Chandler Publishing Company.

Lamon, Michele (2002). *Working Men: Morality and the Boundaries of Race, Class, and Immigration.* Cambridge, MA: Harvard University Press.

Lazare, Aaron (2004). *On Apology.* New York: Oxford University Press.

Lindholm, Torun (2005). Group-based Biases and Validity in Eyewitness Credibility Judgments: Examining Effects of Witness Ethnicity and Presentation Modality. *Journal of Applied Social Psychology* 35: 1474–1501.

McInerny, D. Q. (2005). *Being Logical: A Guide to Good Thinking.* New York: Random House.

Myers, Gerald E. (1986). *William James: His Life and Thought.* New Haven, CT: Yale University Press.

Morell, Virginia (1998). A New Look at Monogamy. *Science* 281 (September 25): 181–2.

Morreall, John (ed.) (1987). *The Philosophy of Laughter and Humor.* New York: The State University of New York Press.

Olson, Steve (2007). Who's Your Daddy? *The Atlantic* (July/August): 36–7.

Pareti, Samisoni (2003). Cannibals' Descendents Offer Apology in 1867 Death. *The New York Times*, November 14.

Phillips, Bob (1998). *The Best Ever Book of Good Clean Jokes.* New York: Galahad Books.

Rescher, Nicholas (1995). *Luck: The Brilliant Randomness of Everyday Life.* New York: Farrar, Straus, and Giroux.

Richardson, Robert D. (2006). *William James: In the Maelstrom of American Modernism.* Boston: Houghton Mifflin.

Skultans, Vieda (1975). *Madness and Morals: Ideas on Insanity in the Nineteenth Century.* London: Routledge & Kegan Paul.

Stearns, Peter N. (1989). *Jealousy: The Evolution of an Emotion in American History.* New York: New York University Press.

Tapper, Albert and Press, Peter (2000). *A Minister, a Priest, and a Rabbi.* Kansas City: Andrews McMeel Publishing.

Trevor-Roper, Patrick (1988). *The World Through Blunted Sight.* London: Penguin Press.

Watzlawick, Paul, Bavelas, J. B., and Jackson, D. D. (1967). *Pragmatics of Human Communication*. New York: W. W. Norton.

Whyte, Jamie (2005). *Crimes against Logic*. New York: McGraw-Hill.

Wolfenstein, Martha (1954). *Children's Humor*. New York: The Free Press.

Wood, Mary Elene (1994). *The Writing on the Wall: Women's Autobiography and the Asylum*. Urbana, IL: University of Illinois Press.

Index